Laughter, *Joy &* Healing

Donald E. Demaray

Light and Life
communications

LAUGHTER, JOY & HEALING
by Donald E. Demaray

ISBN 0-89367-197-5

©1995 Light and Life Press
Second Printing 1998
Light and Life Communications
Indianapolis, IN 46253-5002
Printed in the U.S.A.

*"It must never be forgotten
that joy is one of the commonest
New Testament words."*
— William Barclay

*"It is the heart that is unsure of
his God that is afraid to laugh."*
— George MacDonald

This book I joyously dedicate to
my grandchildren:
Christopher,
Kathleen,
Matthew,
Shawn,
all happy Christians, ready for
a good laugh
at the drop of a hat.

CONTENTS

CREDITS

For those who made research and writing possible, and to others who assisted in advancing this project, I must express gratitude. To Dr. John Van Valin, publisher of Light and Life Press, I want to say warm thanks for consistent encouragement in print ministry, and more particularly for assistance in this book project. To Dr. Kenneth Kinghorn, Provost of Asbury Theological Seminary at the time I began the manuscript, and to Dr. Melvin Dieter, a later Provost, I must express thanks. To Dr. David McKenna, President Emeritus of the Seminary, who has encouraged and suggested, I owe further appreciation. Nor can I forget faculty colleagues, most particularly Dr. Fred Layman, who took time to chat and point me to helpful books and articles. I wish also to thank the Seminary Faculty Research Committee, Administration and Board of Trustees for giving permission for a sabbatical, without which the original book could not have come to birth.

The libraries that provided sources of information include the following: The British Museum, London, where I always find happy and eager assistance. The public library in Pietermaritzburg, South Africa, along with the resources of the Evangelical Biblical Seminary of South Africa, also in Pietermaritzburg, deserve recognition. The Asbury Theological Seminary Library, and especially Mrs. Eunice Weldon, a research librarian, along with John Seery and Dorothy James, also in research assistance, provided aid as often as requested, and always with joy. The community library in North Myrtle Beach, SC, as well as the Myrtle Beach Library, gave me assistance. The central public library at Lexington, KY, provided further help, as did the Jessamine County Library, Nicholasville, KY.

To my wife, Kathleen, and my father, C. Dorr Demaray, for manuscript reading and counsel, I must express thanks. For my children, Cherith, Elyse and James, and the grandchildren, Matthew, Kathleen, Shawn and Christopher, I owe a special debt of gratitude, as I do my son-in-law, Paul Davenport and my daughter-in-law, Charlene Demaray, for the rich resources of family life and ongoing humor they make available. Martin Luther believed the family was a laboratory for learning about life; he hit the nail on the head.

I must thank secretaries Harriet Cook, Harriet Norris and Brook Thelander, all of whom took active interest in the project and did yeoman's service.

I want finally to thank Baker Book House for permission to publish this revised edition of *Laughter, Joy & Healing*.

PREFACE

*"Do not let your hearts
be troubled"* (John 14:1, NRSV).

*"Be of good cheer, I have overcome
the world"* (John 16:33, NKJV).

— *Jesus*

She must take her life. She could no longer tolerate her clinical depression. Then it happened. She fell against the TV, accidentally turning it on. Who should appear on the screen but humorist Art Buchwald. He talked about his own adult depression. Depression so severe he entered the hospital twice.

Reasons — after his birth his mother had to go to a mental home and Art then went to an orphanage. He lived in orphanages for years, and that early conditioning without the presence of biological parents factored into his illness in later life.

But he came through the acute sadness a better, stronger man, and he declared that people in the throes of confusion, chaos and fog must hang on. They would get better.

Well, that woman took courage, and later when she did indeed mend told Art about it. You can believe Art felt in his heart the glow that showed on his face.

Laughter, Art believes, helps us cope with life. In fact, human beings *must* laugh to maintain balance and healthy perspective. The ability to get tickled at the incongruous, and thereby get a handle on living in freedom, evidently is unique to human beings.

This uniqueness helps explain Dr. William Menninger of Menninger Clinic fame, when he declared,

"Your mental health will be better if you have lots of fun outside that office." It also helps interpret Abraham Lincoln who used his sense of humor to cope with incomparably difficult challenges, including a mentally unbalanced wife and a civil war.

Lincoln became famous for admitting he had to pray, for he had no place to go but to God. God gave him a sense of humor, part of the answer to Lincoln's prayers. President Lincoln even told his over-serious government leaders in Washington not only that the stress and strain of the war could keep him in bondage, but that comedy kept him sane. He would perish without the relief that comes with jokes and howling laughter. The government leaders, he declared, had better laugh or risk their own souls.

Spiritually, humor restores perspectives on faith — a major purpose of this book — and thus plays its role in making prayer and creative living true and meaningful. I aim to help people in the struggle of life to rise to *overcoming* and productive faith. Because daily challenges make us busy people, I designed this book for easy reading and reflection in this way. Readings, one for each day over 13 weeks (one quarter of a year), require only five or six minutes. All will inspire and inform. Themes, each time seen through fresh lenses, make clear principles often overlooked but essential for wholeness and fulfilled living.

Donald E. Demaray
Asbury Theological Seminary
The Thanksgiving Season

I

Laughter Therapy

*"Humor is the miracle drug
with no bad side effects."*

— Laurence J. Peter

Have a Good Laugh

On a beautiful spring day in Seattle when the Bing cherry tree was covered with white blossoms, my young son, James, said, "Look mom! The cherry tree's covered with popcorn."

Cherith, my 3-year-old, asked her mother Kathleen permission to invite the little girl next door to play in the sandbox. Kathleen could see the two small ones from the kitchen window. Presently the 3-year-old from next door asked Cherith, "Is your daddy really a doctor?"

Cherith's answer has become part of the family's "joke" file, "Yep," she said, "he's the kind that can't help anybody."

The Scientific Practice of Laughter

"A cheerful heart is a good medicine," says the writer of Proverbs, "but a downcast spirit dries up the bones" (Proverbs 17:22, NRSV). Norman Cousins' laughter-and-healing discoveries of some years ago continue to stick to our ribs. Public figures refer to them; university professors review the findings for their students; and medical colleagues teach them. Cousins discovered for himself the wisdom outlined in the book of Proverbs.

Cousins tells his story in some detail in the celebrated volume, *Anatomy of an Illness as Perceived by the Patient: Reflections on Healing and Regeneration.* His account in summary goes like this. He flew home from overseas, suffering some fever and dull pain. Within a few days he could only move his neck, arms, hands, fingers and legs with difficulty. Tests showed he had a collagen disease. Collagen is the fibrous material holding cells together. "In a sense, then, I was coming unstuck," says Cousins. "Nodules appeared on my body, gravel-like substances under the skin. ..." His chances for recovery? One in 500!

Taking initiative and with the support of his doctors, Cousins studied and learned from the medical literature that he sustained adrenal exhaustion brought on by tension. In effect, negative emotions had changed his body chemistry for the worse. Naturally he asked, can positive thought alter chemistry for the better? He soon got his answer. First he found that nearly all medicines given him in the hospital acted as blockages to healing. He needed to activate his endocrine system, that is, get his immune powers to combat the disease. He proceeded to experiment, and he made significant breakthroughs.

His firsthand detective work taught him that faith, the will to live, hope — in other words an upbeat attitude — related to pain reduction. Cousins also traced the vitamin C connection, massive doses really helped, though surely as important was his frame of mind. Refusing to get caught in the trap of hopelessness, he engineered a program of laughter. Funny movies, hilarious stories and the determination to laugh instead of cry, brought him an amazing realization: "... ten minutes of genuine belly laughter had an anesthetic effect and would give me at least two hours of pain-free sleep." Sedimentation rate testing proved that his laughter episodes not only produced lowered sed-rate readings at the time, but that the whole merriment procedure yielded a cumulative benefit. He was getting better. "I was greatly elated by the discovery that there is a physiological basis for the ancient theory that laughter is good medicine," Norman Cousins concluded. He recovered.

Laughter the Healing Friend

"A cheerful heart," says the biblical writer, "has a continual feast" (Proverbs 15:15b, NRSV). Norman Cousins met another physical challenge more than 15 years after winning over the collagen disease. He tells all in *The Healing Heart: Antidotes to Panic and Helplessness.*

Cousins, far too busy with lecturing and touring to satisfy his body's requirements for exercise and rest, suffered a massive heart attack. Poor diet also contributed to his health problems.

Wisely, he refused to panic. Panic, he observed, constricted the blood vessels. So, remaining calm and confident, he instructed the ambulance driver not to turn on the siren and to drive at normal speed — in other words, to refuse the mood of emergency. In this way, he testified, the trip to the hospital spared him the unusual "strenuous heroics."

As Professor of Medical Humanities at the University of California at Los Angeles School of Medicine, Cousins would tell doctors and medical technologists to recognize that, "Reassurance is the first order of treatment," not histrionics, when people confront physical crisis.

"... de-escalate the usual emergency mood," he instructed wisely.

Once in the hospital setting, Cousins asked for the same unagitated treatment. No waking him in the night for medication which he worked out with his doctor. But his physician leveled with Cousins: "No laughing. You, yourself have said laughing is a form of internal jogging. You're not up to any jogging right now. ... Stay flat on your back and just be a vegetable." Cousins wondered if his condition was worse than the doctor intimated earlier.

Shortly after this "lecture," his wife, Ellen, entered the hospital room. Norman reported the doctor's orders — no laughing, "something I had little practice in doing. ..." But Mrs. Cousins read the day's issue of *The Los Angeles Times* to her husband, and one of the stories struck him so funny that he let out a great roar of laughter, causing nurses to come running. As it turned out, the mirth had done no damage at all. "Right then, I knew I was going to make it all the way. Laughter was still a friend."

3 The Therapeutic Power of a Laughfest

St. Paul put his finger on a thoroughly practical life principle when he said from his prison cell, "Rejoice in the Lord always; again I will say, Rejoice" (Philippians 4:4, NRSV). But we cannot interpret naively the law Paul so succinctly articulated. Some communicators leave the impression that we can laugh our way through and out of illness. Many people see laughter as a metaphor for the entire range of positive emotions — hope, faith, love, the will to live, cheer, humor, creativity, playfulness, confidence, great expectations. The bottom line being that positive thoughts form a solid base for getting well.

The psychologist Thomas W. Allen, a professor at Washington University (St. Louis), says "Our thoughts reverberate in our bodies." That means that for every positive thought, our bodies register a corresponding physiological reaction for the good.

Mr. Cousins, knowing of the current move toward organized laughfests in hospitals as a factor in enhancing the curative effects of medical therapies, took on an assignment at the Sepulveda Veterans Administration Hospital in California. At the first meeting about 50 people assembled. Cousins reviewed brain research findings, focusing on glandular activity. He went on to detail benefits of laughing. William Fry, Jr. of Stanford's School of Medicine had itemized benefits, including greater respiration. Laughter builds a roadblock to panic and apprehension and frees up the body's healing systems, Cousins concluded.

After his stimulating thoughts, Cousins engaged patients, along with doctors and nurses, in an experiment. They would create an atmosphere of laughter. And laugh they did. They laughed at stories and jokes; they laughed during the playing of a cassette laugh track. Contagion set in, and the audible mirth could hardly be stopped. After ten minutes, Cousins asked how they felt. For some, pain had lessened, showing perhaps that the body's endorphins (natural painkillers) had gone to work.

The next step was natural. The patients would set up their own programs of joke sharing, comedians on video — anything and everything to get people to laugh. The patients cooperated with the result that a fellowship of participation was established, and that opened the door to progress reports weekly. The laughfest meetings pleased the physicians, not only because of the changed mood of the patients, but also because of their physical improvement.

Doctors Prescribe Laughter

Jesus, the Great Physician, declared the intended result of His teachings: "... that my joy may be in you, and that your joy may be complete" (John 15:11, NRSV). An expression of that joy is a spirit of mirth.

Mark Twain intuited what modern science now documents. In *Tom Sawyer*, he tells about the old man who "laughed loud and joyously, shook up the details of his anatomy from head to foot, and ended by saying that such a laugh was money in a man's pocket, because it cut down the doctor's bills like everything."

A researcher for the Nurses for Laughter organization discovered that humorous nurses lend a sense of well-being to patients, speed up their adjustment to the hospital setting and drain off worry. No wonder laughter programs emerge in hospitals and doctors actually prescribe mirth.

Johns Hopkins Hospital shows humorous films from Candid Camera to the Three Stooges on closed circuit TV. Patients at Wilcox Memorial in Hawaii enjoy the benefits of stand-up comics who make videos; these professionals do their work *gratis*. At a Catholic hospital in Texas, nuns tell funny stories to every patient on a daily basis!

Today, clowns go into mental hospitals and cancer wards and also perform before cardiac patients. Some patients actually are cured, cancer victims enter recession periods and the general tone of well-being rises. Healthcare and social-work professionals pay hefty registration fees to enroll in a conference or workshop on laughter and play.

Actually, what flowers in the literature and lecturing on play and fun, is that life itself requires the jocular. Without glee, we live unfulfilled lives. Adults often lose this ability, even feel guilty about engaging in fun. ("I really ought to do something important," we reason.)

The *Seattle Times* summed it up nicely: "Health professionals have long known that play and positive attitudes can help heal. In recent years, scientists also have begun to document the complex chemical changes that occur in the body as a result of both pleasure and stress." And *The Indianapolis Star* carried a tiny article entitled, "Laugh Yourself to Health." "Doctors report increasing evidence," the piece began, "that a person can laugh himself to health." The article continues: "The November issue of *Science Digest* cites several studies in which laughter produced beneficial physical and mental results." Moreover, "A hearty laugh benefits lungs and clears the respiratory system," the researchers said.

A Safety Valve

Gerald Piaget, one of the founders of the Institute for the Advancement of Human Behavior and a professor of psychiatry at Stanford University, says humor that exposes the incongruities of life can provide safety valves for conflict. The Laughter Project at the University of California, Santa Barbara, carried out research that showed laughter reduced stress just as efficiently as expensive biofeedback training. Try to beat that! No fees for a program, no equipment or lab — just the merriment human beings can generate.

Hans Selye, father of modern stress research, documented chemical and biological factors in tension-oriented situations — adrenal enlargement, weight loss and increase of corticoids in the blood to list a few. The great Canadian doctor learned that adrenal exhaustion can erupt from emotional involvements like frustration, disappointment and hidden and suppressed angers. He went on to find that this kind of energy depletion is really distress; stress itself does us good, because it forms the launching pad for getting things done.

So the practical question emerges, how can I live with wholesome stress, avoiding distress? The *Wellness Letter* of the University of California at Berkley, gives us an answer in one long but delightful sentence: "Certainly a good, old-fashioned thigh-slapper can be a real workout, raising body temperature about a half a degree, setting the whole cardiovascular system pulsating, throwing the abdominal, lumbar, internal intercostal, subcostal, and transverse thoracic muscles into gear, rocking the glottis and larynx, rumbling up the windpipe, and banging against the trachea to emerge, finally, in a burst of mirth that sometimes issues from a person at a speed of 70 miles an hour, followed by muscle relaxation." Hilarity causes muscle contractions in the abdomen, chest, shoulders and an increase in heart, respiration and blood pressure rates. After the laughter episodes, muscles relax and heart and blood pressure pace dip even below normal.

As Proverbs 12:25 (NRSV) points out: "Anxiety weighs down the human heart, but a good word cheers it up." The safety valve called laughter releases us to gladness and restores normalcy.

Endorphins and All That

Jesus said we should "be of good cheer" (John 16:33, RSV). The good cheer He made possible ingrains itself into our very bodies. An American Medical Association bulletin carried the research finding that every organ of the body responds to laughter — reacts to the good!

In a telling article in *American Health*, Robert Brody details the body's response to a good hee-haw. The pituitary gland shoots out endorphins, chemical cousins of painkilling drugs like heroin and morphine. The lacrimal glands of the eyes produce tears. The zygomatic muscles in the head contort as if in pain. The lower jaw vibrates lickety-bang. The arteries relax after tensing. Vocal cords undergo spasm and produce sound. The heart increases its pace, meeting immediate oxygen needs. Lungs build pressure before releasing air. The diaphragm tightens for spasms of respiration. From the nervous system comes a deluge of adrenaline which issues in euphoria. Abdominal muscles double like a fist. Leg muscles relax, causing a weakening feeling.

Gelotology, which is the study of laughter, derived from the Greek prefix *gelos* for laughter, finds itself only in the preliminary stages of isolating laughter's benefits.

We already suspect pain-oriented diseases like arthritis can benefit. We know for a fact that both mental pain, such as depression and physical distress reduce; that blood flow enhances; and that digestion improves.

Dr. William F. Fry, Jr., a leading gelotologist of our time, reveals that laughter initiates "a massive brain reaction." Fry also learned that happy people may laugh up to 400 times a day. Put that all together and see that physical and psychological catharsis induced by hearty mirth helps explain the peace and good health many people enjoy.

A College Dedicated to Laughter

Clowns make us laugh, and laughter relieves stress. The Barnum and Bailey Clown College, Venice, Florida, spends a tidy sum (several thousand dollars, actually) to train each student, who pays only for his or her keep, in a ten week course. Seasoned clowns do the teaching. Why all the effort and expenditure? Clowns, cross-cultural and worldwide, come with no prejudice, no preconceived idea about the way you ought to think and live. Distrust and credibility gaps don't show up in their world. Clowns make an unfriendly world into a friendly one. The emotional release in us who watch them perform rises above calculation.

Today clowns perform in churches and hospitals, as well as at the circus. They make people laugh on street corners and in rest homes. Who can know whether or not any researcher will ever document the full range of therapeutic effects? But we do know that a harlequin's face reads like a humor book, and that circus pantomime (professional clowns generally do not talk) tickles our funny bones. These jovial pranksters, perhaps above all other comedians, have the ability to divert attention.

P.T. Barnum intuited that clowns make up the heart of the circus. In 1871 when Barnum and two partners started the circus, now known as the Ringling Brothers and Barnum and Baily Circus, clowns learned through on-the-job training. A more recent owner, Irvin Feld, established the Clown College to give more formal shape to the education of aspiring buffoons. Schoolwork begins in the fall while the circus makes preparation for a new season. The students must master juggling, gymnastics, stilts, makeup and costume creation. No one under 17 years of age may enter the college.

One young clown testifies, "When I see somebody laughing at me, I love it. It feels really good." Some have gone so far as to compare Christ and clowns. We can trust Jesus and He can make people laugh (see Elton Trueblood's *The Humor of Christ*). "I came," said our Lord, "that they may have life, and have it abundantly" (John 10:10b, NRSV).

II

Sources of Joy, Laughter and Life

"Keep company with the more cheerful sort of the godly; there is no mirth like the mirth of believers."

— Richard Baxter

Have a Good Laugh

Sir Winston Churchill was accosted by a mean spirited woman who said to him, "I hate you. If you were my husband, I would poison your tea."

Without missing a beat, Sir Winston replied, "Madam, if you were my wife, I'd drink it."

The Resurrection Connection

Ecclesiastes 3:3 (RSV) refers to a "time to weep, and a time to laugh; a time to mourn, and a time to dance." Notice the sequence. Winter comes before spring, grief before joy, death prior to resurrection.

In the early history of the Greek Orthodox Church,

1

an interesting custom developed. The day after Easter, ministers and lay persons went to church to tell funny stories! Yes, jokes and tales of hilarity. These ancient people had their reason. They must celebrate the enormous prank God played on the devil. Jesus rose victorious over the grave!

This almost overpowering feeling of relief characterizes true Christians. Stanley Jones used to say he didn't grieve over the awful events in life very long simply because he knew how it would all turn out. The resurrection documents that God, not evil, stands in charge of life.

Why, then, do so many church members feel and look like somber, Good Friday Christians? One wonders if certain influential fathers of the church set in motion a chain reaction.

One great preacher of long ago actually did a sermon opposing laughter. Preaching at the end of the fourth century, he saw jollity as pagan. He declared that Christians must focus on their sins, that God doesn't want His children to play, and that if the devil can get people engaged in frivolity he's won the day.

Actually, many leading preachers through the centuries have embraced that very position. But it's wrong, for it rests on premises far from the joy characteristic of the early followers of Christ. In fact, if Christianity had begun under the sponsorship of that kind of thinking, it would have died a natural death. For, you see, the indisputable fact of the resurrection accounts for the church, its persistence, its liberated vitality and therefore its radiant witness.

2 That Grand Parenthesis

Beginnings and endings in Scripture instruct us. The first words of Genesis, "In the beginning God," come across with as much positive thrust as the "grace of the Lord Jesus" benediction closing the book of Revelation. The Acts of the Apostles commences with Jesus' life and work, and terminates with that liberating word "unhin-dered." The story of our Lord in the Gospels begins with a marriage feast and concludes with His resurrection.

A great deal in between beginnings and endings, however, relates to sin and the horrors of evil. The book of Psalms, for example, faces our inclination toward iniq-uity. Yet notice the first and last clauses of the book of Psalms: "Blessed are those ..." and "Praise the Lord!" This does not imply a facile evaluation of life, for the full scope of human emotions and behaviors finds expression in the body of the Psalter. But to read through all 150 psalms over and again yields this clear finding that the dominant expression is praise.

This framework of joy characterizes those who iden-tify with the Judeo-Christian tradition. Jesus could eat and drink with publicans and sinners, because he lived above the meanness of the world. He lived beyond it, enjoying life to the fullest, and therefore possessed the clear perspective necessary for helping publicans and sinners.

Professor Conrad Hyers of Gustavus Adolphus College in Minnesota, talks about the "grand parenthe-sis" in which Jesus did His work. The feast at Cana be-gins His ministry; the festivals of Easter and Pentecost bring it to a close. He never hid from pain and the cross or from the renunciation and abandonment He suffered (even by His family). But the Lord knew His origin! He knew His destiny! This explains His unrelenting talk about abundant life, hope, faith, cheer and a hundred more positives.

Jesus' followers know their beginnings; their cre-ation in God. They keep going by the inspired vision of their debarkation point. And that explains the joy of Christ's disciples. No wonder Elton Trueblood could say over dinner with friends, "Isn't it fun to be a Christian!"

3

Freedom to Live and Laugh

St. Paul tells us salvation comes through faith, not law. Law imprisons; grace frees. The Christian's laugh may well express a deeply settled sense of inner freedom.

Herein lies a Christian truth which has its spinoffs in today's society. For example, jails in Missouri discovered cartoons as an instrument of prisoner rehabilitation. Humor, prison authorities discovered, opens windows on defining and solving personal problems.

Another example, the Ethel Percy Andrus Gerontology Center in Los Angeles developed a humor handbook. It includes comedy tape lists, funny movies, limericks, bibliographies, cartoons and anything to unbind the spirit of the confined.

Peter Berger, insightful writer of our day, declares that, "The comic reflects the imprisonment of the human spirit in the world." Humor points to transcendence, to emancipation. Just try to bottle up human beings, especially Christians who know their freedom in Christ!

We all suffer temptation to succumb to negatives. Pettiness, for example. But humor acts as a great antidote, emancipating us to live above the trivial. Often pettiness comes garbed in pomposity and bombast, but God's gift of humor documents our ability to make pretense transparent. And jocularity also helps us see our own pretentious behavior. Isn't that part of the genius of laughing at ourselves?

A true theology of play tells us not to take ourselves and circumstances too seriously. Kierkegaard said we should connect with the relative relatively, and relate to the absolute absolutely. Released laughter and wholesome play restore vision and give us the freedom to distinguish between the relative and the absolute and to shape thought and behavior accordingly.

The Christian knows the source of laughter: Rock-of-Gibraltar faith. After all, God stands bigger than the details of our lives and the problems that threaten to plague us. The more one believes in the sovereignty of God, the greater the freedom to enjoy God's world and even to laugh at life's contradictions.

Paul said, "I ... died to the law" (Galatians 2:19, NRSV). Honest-to-goodness freedom is reason enough to have a good laugh. Who can stop the flow of mirth from an unshackled spirit?

The God of Surprises

4

Surprise often triggers laughter. Surprise comes from God Himself. He made us for delight in the unexpected.

The grandest of all purely human surprises is the knowledge of sins forgiven. God even forgets our sins, promising never to remember them. He assures us that though our sins are "like scarlet, they shall be as white as snow; though they are red like crimson, they shall become like wool" (Isaiah 1:18, RSV).

Concert singer David Baker publicly gives his testimony of conversion. He had lived with drugs and in deep sin. Then one day, an old college classmate began working with David and led him to Christ. Says Dave, "The joy! The sheer joy and reality of Christ! I just can't get over it all." The delight of his words matches the smile on his face like a child seeing lighted candles on a birthday cake.

The sense of release that comes with forgiveness is enormous. But God's surprises don't stop there. Right through life He delights us with the unexpected, sometimes by His special presence. Sunday night, sitting in church, I listened to the testimony of a mother who praised God, through tears, because her children live in the kingdom. God came to me in that moment. I smiled. One always does when God comes like that.

Seminarians, nearly all of them, live with money problems. But they cannot resist smiling, even laughing, when they rehearse God's need-meeting provisions. One fellow finds money from an anonymous donor under the door to his dormitory room; another locates a job; still one more hears from his home church. Surprise always knocks, comes in and laughs.

The very nature of a joke is tension followed by release. Begin to listen to a story and your muscles actually tighten. Tensity accelerates in anticipation of the anecdote's funny ending. A giggle or two documents your anticipation before the climax. Finally comes the guffaw, fulfillment of your internal wishes to hear something genuinely comical. Hope vindicates itself by the surprising close to the story.

Unlike a "funny" story that doesn't quite come off, Christians foresee life's culmination in authentic hope. Hope centers in God, unmovable and sure. The hope in God holds surprises we cannot know now.

5 Deliverance

Isaiah, in a moment of jubilant inspiration, prophesied like this, "Seek the Lord while He may be found, call upon Him while He is near; let the wicked forsake their way, and the unrighteous their thoughts; let them return to the Lord, that He may have mercy on them, and to our God, for He will abundantly pardon" (Isaiah 55:6-7, NRSV).

For Basilea Schlink, founder of the Sisters of Mary, Darmstadt, Germany, the secret of the joy-saturated life is repentance. Mother Basilea wrote to a friend that we praise God for many things, "but no exultation on earth can or will surpass the exultation over God's gift of the forgiveness of sins." She concludes that the psalmist's song, *Bless the Lord, O my soul,* "resounds not only here on earth, but throughout the heavenly spheres, for there is joy in heaven over one sinner who repents."

Christians know the experience of deliverance, not only in pardon for sin but from illness, circumstance and rejection. Whenever deliverance comes, and for whatever reason, always the deep relief brings joy to the heart and laughter from the soul. So a criminal writes that though prison bars keep him in jail, he lives "a free man in Christ Jesus. ..." Someone else says, "For the past two weeks I felt as if the corners of my mouth had been permanently tied down so I couldn't laugh or smile and I wondered why." The heaviness deep in her soul yielded to deliverance. Then she said, "... I can smile now and I feel it inside and out. ..."

The *Book of Common Prayer* gathers up, in its 1662 edition, the experience of joy and comfort that comes with the sense of rescue. Note the vivid figures of those in trouble, then the subsequent relief:

> They reel to and fro, and stagger like a
>   drunken man: and are at their wit's end.
> So when they cry unto the Lord in their
>   trouble: he delivereth them out of their distress.
> For he maketh the storm to cease: so that the
>   waves thereof are still.
> Then are they glad, because they are at rest: and
>   so he bringeth them unto the heaven
>   where they would be.

The Spirit of Christ

Jesus said, "The thief comes only to steal and kill and destroy. I came that they may have life, and have it abundantly" (John 10:10, NRSV).

Samuel Logan Brengle, who became perhaps the most remarkable Salvation Army evangelist America produced, testifies to a profound experience of the Spirit of Christ. He had sought a deeper experience of God for some time. One morning, during this searching period, he awakened "hungering and thirsting just to live this life of fellowship with God," he confesses. Getting up at 6:00 a.m., he opened his Bible and read some words of Jesus which "gave me such a blessing as I never had dreamed a man could have this side of heaven." Brengle tries to describe his joy: "It was an unutterable revelation. It was a heaven of love."

Up and dressed, ready to meet the new day, he walked across Boston Common before breakfast, "weeping for joy and praising God. Oh, how I loved! In that hour I knew Jesus, and I loved Him till it seemed my heart would break with love. I was filled with love for all His creatures," he continues touchingly. "I heard the little sparrows chattering; I loved them. I loved the dogs, I loved the horses, I loved the little urchins on the street, I loved the strangers who hurried past me, I loved the heathen — I loved the whole world!"

This reminds one of St. Francis of Assisi who, after he had given his inheritance to God, experienced inexpressible joy. Not everyone, of course, has such ecstatic experience of God's grace. Nor does any Christian, St. Francis and Samuel Logan Brengle included, live on top of the world at all times. After all, the Christian does live by faith in the struggle of life, and in that way builds spiritual muscle.

This one grand truth sings its way into our souls: Resurrection Christians live in the joy of the Lord. Why? The Spirit of the resurrected Lord lives in His people.

7 Hope

Saint Paul gives us a gem of a statement in Romans 15:13, "May the God of hope fill you with all joy and peace in believing, so that you may abound in hope by the power of the Holy Spirit" (NRSV).

On a picture calendar, Canon Bryan Green gives meaningful commentary on Paul's verse: "Joy is the fruit of the Holy Spirit," the distinguished Englishman begins. He goes on to make clear that this happiness is no superficial affair, something to keep us forever free from sadness and suffering. Rather, it is inner confidence in God's love and holding power which "gives a consistent flow of joy deep beneath the waves of trouble and the winds of sorrow." This accounts for the "deep confidence that I am God's forgiven, accepted child and that He will never, never let me go."

Have you noticed how hope and joy go together in Scripture?

Paul says "we rejoice in our hope of sharing the glory of God" (Romans 5:2, RSV).

Isaiah, the prophet of hope, cries, "For you shall go out in joy, and be led forth in peace: the mountains and the hills before you shall break forth into singing, and all the trees of the field shall clap their hands" (55:12, RSV).

The author of Hebrews talks about "looking to Jesus the pioneer and perfecter of our faith, who for the joy that was set before him endured the cross, despising the shame, and is seated at the right hand of the throne of God" (12:2, RSV).

Someone rightly observed that, "Other men see only a hopeless end, but the Christian rejoices in an endless hope." Doesn't that explain Sam Shoemaker's statement, "The surest mark of a Christian is not faith, or even love, but joy"? Hope invades mind and heart with joy; that's a law of the human spirit.

Reverend Feldon gets even with his wife for volunteering
him to speak at the women's tea.

III

Power to Cope

*"... do not be grieved, for the
joy of the Lord is your strength."*
— Nehemiah 8:10, NRSV

Have a Good Laugh
A Child's View of Retired Life

*After summer recess, a teacher asked her pupils how
they spent their vacations. Here's one small boy's reply:*

We always spent vacations with Grandma and
Grandpa. They used to live here in the North in a big
brick house, but grandpa got retarded and they moved
down South to Del Ray Beach. They now call themselves
retardees. They ride big three-wheeled tricycles. They go
to a building they call the wrecked hall, but if it was
wrecked, it has now been fixed. They play games there,
watch videos, do exercises and talk a lot. They only talk
about three things: how sick they are, how much they can
sell their condos for, and where they can get the cheapest
early bird. I don't know what an early bird is, but all the
retardees love them.

Behind the wrecked hall is a swimming pool and they go in it, but they don't swim. They just stand in the water up to their bellies, with their hats on.

My grandma used to bake cookies and stuff, but I guess she forgot how because nobody cooks there. They all go to restaurants — usually at 4:00 in the afternoon. I'm not used to eating supper that early, but grandpa says, "The early bird catches the worm." Who wants to eat worms??? Yuk!

As you come into the retardee park, there is a dollhouse with a man sitting in it. He watches all the retardees all day long so they can not get out without seeing him. They all have badges with their names on them. I guess they do not know who they are unless they look at their badges.

My grandma says grandpa worked hard all his life and has earned his retardment. I wish they would move back North, but I guess the man in the dollhouse won't let them go.

Author unknown
Taken from *Psychology for Living*,
September-October 1994.

1 Energy

In a historic moment when God's people found themselves tempted to embrace regret, Nehemiah counseled, "... do not be grieved, for the joy of the Lord is your strength" (Nehemiah 8:10, NRSV). The people obeyed and had a party! In that festive mood they made "great rejoicing" (v. 12).

Sorrow depletes energies; joy replaces them. Restoration starts in the brain, moves to the nervous system, and finally encompasses the whole body. Both the chemical and electrical functions of brain and body get into the act. Laughter kicks the endocrine system into motion. Hormones secrete to give "runner's high." Have you noticed how alert you feel, how vigorous, after a good laugh? You sense the same after brisk and sprightly exercise, like running or swimming.

The hormones, called catecholamines, move into the blood system, and the enhanced circulation generates more laughter and encourages bodily well-being. The pituitary gland functions, and that may activate endorphins and enkephalins, natural painkillers.

That's not all. The brain's right side increases in chemical activity, important because the right hemisphere controls emotions and creativity. Actually, both right and left sides of the brain work together in exceptional harmony when we enter into a happy mood.

Further, a good laugh does something to the fibers of the nervous system. Initiating charges in the brain, laughter generates both electrical and chemical impulses related to the hypothalamus, the message-control center. Messages go to the cerebral cortex, the place where discernment kicks in. Can you help wonder that hard, cognitive problems yield to the fresh energy now in the brain?

The bottom line is that play, fun and laughter feed the entire system, mental and physical, to heighten energy for productivity and efficiency.

A Weapon

Observe the subtle wisdom of Job 3:25: "Truly the thing that I fear comes upon me, and what I dread befalls me" (NRSV). This well-taken warning relates to life the way it happens, for negative thoughts give birth to negative ordeals, but positive thoughts yield positive experiences. Humor is one of God's weapons against worries and the eventualities they inspire.

A hijacker commanded passengers not to make a move; he had a gun. He entered the pilot's area, but a professional comedian got everyone laughing in the hijacker's absence. And when he came back and saw all the people overtly laughing, he concluded they did not take him seriously, lost his nerve, and gave up!

Herman Jose, a Portuguese TV comedian from Lisbon, has great fun with political leaders, but only aims at those who themselves see the funny side of life. In the Reagan days, he observed that, "Reagan tells jokes," but goes on to say, "I leave the Communists alone because they have no sense of humor." Herman knows that laughing people survive and go on to victories. He also knows that those who cannot or will not laugh have already mapped out their doom.

A doctor said of a friend, "He will never have a breakdown because he has a hair-trigger laugh." Likewise, an insightful leader said of a colleague going through the stress of adjusting to retirement, "He laughs easily so I know he will come through this period OK."

Humor documents one's contact with reality. A grip on the facts means mental health which signifies wholeness.

One of the most interesting experiments in laughter research relates to alcoholism. The South African Brain Research Institute uses not conventional heavy sedation therapy, but laughing gas, oxygen and nitrous oxide. After 700 cases treated in the new way, they note the reversal of both physical and psychological withdrawal symptoms and also the shortening of detoxification periods. The success rate stands so high that some with expertise in the field of rehabilitation believe the new treatment will become standard.

We now know body chemistry alters with laughter. It can change our whole psychology. Then clearly, it is a weapon against, and a way of coping with, anxiety and negativity.

3 A Way of Seeing

Humorists win. They win because they can see clearly.

A novelist probably determined the success of his career because he used laughter as an agent for keeping his sight at 20/20. Listen to the way it happened.

As a beginning reporter for a small newspaper, he got a letter from his father who wrote impatiently about his son never amounting to a row of beans. Though annoyed, the young reporter wrote not a blistering reply, but indicated that though at 21 he seemed incapable, he had in fact thought out his life goals. His plan for achievement? At 30, he intended to be a great newspaper reporter; at 40, a great editor; at 50, a great story writer; at 60, a great fiction writer; at 70, a great grandfather; at 80, a great admirer of beautiful women; and at 90, a great loss to the community.

His father had a good laugh. And, significantly, the years saw the son's career proceed along the very lines he predicted in that amusing letter.

I have a friend who refuses to worry, for he knows anxiety fogs his lenses and makes focus impossible. Although my friend has fought big problems for 50 years, he insists on dissipating his fret potential in humor. Riotously funny, he keeps his problems reduced to a size easily seen and puts them in a corner where he can keep a bead on them. He never allows them to tower over him so they can look down from some mocking position. Humor becomes a pair of spectacles through which he sees life whole. This way of seeing holds him to faith and keeps him collected in the long years of his wife's illness.

Says Irving Oyle, a medical doctor, "Positive, beautiful thoughts trigger the release of beneficial hormones in the body and these in turn help the body to heal itself." But, he says, "If you presume that you live in a hostile universe, the reaction to that presumption is what wears out your body."

"Faith," Dr. Oyle concludes, "creates the hormones that make you live longer."

And what generates faith? Prayer, affirmative thinking, positive achievement, and of course, humor. How do you look at your world? If through hostile, paranoid eyes, you can change your prescription, God being your Ophthalmologist.

Rising to Challenges

Abraham Lincoln, though given a great and godly vision for America, suffered as many failures as any person in our history. He tried farming and failed; he attempted to make a living by commercial water transport and failed; he made an effort at teaching school and failed. Even his marriage proved tragic. He ran for public office time and again, failing more often than not. And when, at last, he won the presidency he inherited a war.

Any ordinary person would have given up. Not Lincoln. Humor, prayer and a fine mind kept him alive and thinking clearly. During the nonstop disasters of the Civil War, this lanky, towering human being walked the midnight corridors of the White House in his red flannel nightwear, hoping to find someone still awake, someone with whom he could share a funny tale from his reading. Reporters tell us he had a laugh like the neigh of a wild horse, a laugh which became famous for its hearty and full-bodied character.

In a tense board meeting, the wise executive will not beat his head against a stone wall, but create an opening in the atmosphere with wit and humor. A funny story or pleasant aside will come as welcome relief, clear minds and forward problem solving.

Much of the same psychology pertains when we watch a thriller on TV. The commercials come every 14 minutes or so and do more than advertise. They bring comic relief. They say, "All's normal after all," a message necessary for the restoration of perspective.

Wholesome laughter indicates that the one doing the laughing enjoys self-respect and healthy faith. It says of a leader, especially one going through the throes of defeating the odds against him, that he can, after all, do his job. Laughter says you believe in yourself, and that helps others believe in you.

Let laughter reign when it comes. It is oil for the engines that rise to challenges and work miracles.

Laughing Toward Old Age

5

Researchers have come to two delightful conclusions from their studies of laughter: joy encourages longevity and also contributes to quality of life in geriatrics.

Laughter increases respiration, aids oxygen exchange and heightens muscular activity. It contributes to a better functioning cardiovascular system, does the same for the sympathetic nervous system, and sets off the body's own pain-lessening enzymes. Beta-endorphins come to production, and some believe they create that good feeling we all have when we laugh wholeheartedly.

Like physical exercise, laughter reduces depression, stress and hypertension, all key challenges for most human beings including older people. With emotional and physical therapy comes potential for minimizing the possibility of strokes and heart attacks, ulcers and chronic headaches and a host of other ailments.

Dr. Jeffrey Goldstein, a psychologist at Temple University, Philadelphia, speaks forthrightly about the definite possibility that laughter relates "in several ways to longevity." That news gets around quickly.

In fact, the American Association of Retired Persons (AARP) engaged their members in a humor ideas project. It started with a letter to the *AARP News Bulletin* written by Ethel Wise of Atlanta. "I am a volunteer trying to bring laughter to residents of nursing homes and patients in hospitals or hospices," she wrote. "I urge your members to send along their suggestions ... because my people are waiting to laugh." The response surprised, even amazed her. From every state in the Union, and other areas around the world like Australia and the Virgin Islands, letters came daily.

"This enormous response has restored my faith in mankind," she commented.

Cards, tapes, cartoon scrapbooks, magazines and books all appeared in the mail. Creative suggestions came galore: entertainment from service clubs like the Lions and Kiwanis; joke notebooks for looking at or reading aloud; ideas for getting help from a public library; how to use high school/college groups and community choirs, too.

People intuit that cheer is a good doctor. In fact, Tom Mullen, in *Laughing Out Loud and Other Religious Experiences*, says that, "Specialists in gerontology have observed that healthy, very elderly patients invariably demonstrate a spirit of fun."

6 Taking Life in Good Humor

St. Paul exhorts us to have no anxiety, not even about little things. George Burns, in *How to Live to Be One Hundred — or More*, teaches us some things about minimizing anxiety. "If you ask me what is the single-most important key to longevity, I would have to say it is avoiding worry, stress and tension. And if you didn't ask me," old George concludes wryly, "I'd still have to say it."

So he wrote a book to help us. He outlines his exercise program — the Knee-Hi, the Pedal Pusher, the Neck Stretcher. ... He has fun with his dietary pattern — prunes comes in as a breakfast favorite — but the bottom line is that he eats very little. He helps us avoid negatives by exhorting that if we expect to reach age 100 we need to have a positive attitude. "Even if you're going to fail, be positive about it. That way you'll be a successful failure."

Toward the end of his book he talks about death in a chapter called, "Stay Away from Funerals, Especially Yours." George cautions against looking in the obituary column: if your name doesn't appear there, go ahead and have breakfast. If he himself ever finds his name in the column, "I'd still have breakfast. I'm not leaving on an empty stomach." Even after brain surgery at 98, he kidded the nurses!

Whether the famous comedian knows it or not, he advocates a system of good health under the metaphor of humor. The eminently wholesome attitude he projects much of the time does great good for people of any age; his comments become "a priceless guide to levity and longevity which will have you charging on to 100 — and laughing all the way."

Comedians Help Us Cope

7

The psalmist exhorts us to do away with our fears. "I sought the Lord, and he answered me, and delivered me from all my fears" (Psalms 34:4, NRSV). Then the poet gives us the clue: "Look to him [the Lord] and be radiant; so your faces shall never be ashamed" (v. 5).

Francis Schaeffer believed that radiant witness lies, at least in part, in what he called the Christian's "beauty." I agree. But the way to lose that glow is to take ourselves and the world too seriously. Cartoonists and comedians use their art to release us from that seriousness; they poke fun at our wrinkled brows and in so doing translate wrinkles into smiles.

Will Rogers knew that having fun, say at the government's expense, may do us about as much good as coming up with solutions. "I don't make jokes," he commented with his Oklahoma cowboy wit, "I just watch the government and report what I see."

Bill Cosby's great gift is to help us handle reality — the tensions of daily family life, for example, which he reduces to size. His tone calls up, in each of us, the child within, and children see life through unencumbered eyes and find ways of managing it.

Jack Benny was "the sucker," and Jackie Gleason was "the helpless one." All comedians work with tragedy, the basic stuff of comedy. When any impossible situation hangs like a specter, human beings find relief in a valve called humor.

Thus Steve Allen comments, "To look purposely for the element of humor in an uncomfortable situation is to make use of an important procedure in emotional control, in the maintenance of one's own mental health. We sometimes joke and laugh," he concludes, "because we do not wish to fight or destroy ourselves."

Thank God for the humorists who take away our sadness, a great drain on energies. They prove themselves God's instruments helping us cope with life and restoring radiance, the hallmark of vigor and vitality.

IV

Worship and Joy

*"When Christian worship
is dull and joyless,
Jesus Christ has been left outside —
that is the only possible explanation."*
— James S. Stewart

Have a Good Laugh

Leighton Ford, a happy preacher, has had lots of fun over his relationship to Billy Graham, his brother-in-law. Some call him Mr. Graham's son-in-law, even mother-in-law and sister-in-law.

Presenting Leighton Ford to collegians in chapel, a presiding educator twisted his tongue to everyone's delight: "We are happy to have Leighton Ford as our speaker this morning," he commenced by way of introduction. "Perhaps some of you don't know that Leighton Ford is married to Billy Graham's brother."

Tittering all around. But the distinguished presenter, unaware of his error and non-pulsed by audience response, added, "That makes Leighton, Billy Graham's son-in-law."

Now the students could not help but roll in the aisles. The usually careful public speaker, trying desperately to mend what must have gone wrong, only fell completely into a comedy of errors by concluding, "So ... now I present to you, Leighton Ford's brother-in-law, Billy Graham!"

1 Joy in God's House

Isaiah, prophesying in the name of the Lord, speaks of those who identify with authentic religion. "... these I will bring to my holy mountain," says God through His servant, "and make them joyful in my house of prayer" (Isaiah 56:7, NRSV).

On the surface, it would seem St. Paul disagreed with Isaiah, for Paul warns the Ephesians against levity which, he says, is not fitting (Ephesians 5:4). St. Benedict cautioned monks against laughter, and another monk who lived a long time ago, Peter Damiani, claimed laughter the most difficult of offenses to eradicate.

But Benedict and Damiani suffered an exegetical conditioning that blinded them from seeing writers like St. Paul in context. Later in that fifth chapter of Ephesians, Paul exhorts worshiping Christians to address "one another in psalms and hymns and spiritual songs, singing and making melody to the Lord with all your heart ..." (5:19, RSV). Martin Luther evidently read Paul in context, for he declared with a lot of conviction that "it is pleasing to the dear God whenever thou rejoicest or laughest from the bottom of thy heart." And one suspects that this introducer of joyous singing into the Christian church did not resist laughing out loud in church.

Back to Paul and levity, the levity he cried out against. We must remember that levity is boorishness, laughing at the sacred or at something we should treat with respect. We see boors as ill-mannered and uncouth; filth may characterize their speech. By complete contrast we have verse 20 of chapter 5 of Ephesians, where St. Paul gives us the object of our rejoicing, the Lord Jesus Christ. And just there, or rather, just in Him, we find the source of our delight, the Resurrected Christ victorious over all evil.

James S. Stewart rightly declared that, "When Christian worship is dull and joyless, Jesus Christ has been left outside — that is the only possible explanation."

But laughter, actual laughter. Do we give place to that in Christian worship? Yes. Laughter recognizes our finitude in contrast to our ultimate security in Christ. Reinhold Niebuhr says humor is a "prelude to faith," that laughter is "the beginning of prayer" and "a vestibule to the temple of confession." The purpose of worship is the renewal that comes with submission to the One Mightier than ourselves. To catch a glimpse of the omnipotent God in contrast to our limitations may well bring a relieved smile to our lips.

And our security? That comes when we find our confidence in the God who lived in Christ and in us, too. Gordon W. Allport, the Harvard psychologist, makes the astute suggestion that, "A case might be made for the potentially superior humor of the religious person who has settled once and for all what things are of ultimate value, sacred and untouchable. For then nothing else in the world need be taken seriously." Christ does indeed settle value and security.

Clowns Go to Church

Buried deep in the heart of every person lies the necessity of festivity; which relates to why we often refer to worship as "celebration". The Bible talks a great deal about feasts and festivals, especially high sacred occasions. Notice that Hebrews celebrated "to the Lord" (Exodus 5:1, 12:14, etc.).

Festive expression in our day has taken what at first

2

seems a strange turn. The Reverend Floyd Shaffer, a Lutheran minister, sometimes dresses as a clown. He will, for example, preside over Holy Communion services attended by nearly 200 clowns. No, he does not come across sacrilegious, but as an entirely serious celebrant.

Actually, dozens of ministers in very recent years have engaged in clowning as a vehicle of Christian communication. They call themselves "fools for Christ's sake," since God "made foolish the wisdom of the world." Christ showed himself childlike and simple; He enjoyed the everyday experiences of life, believed in everyone's potential. And Jesus did indeed see possibilities in everybody, even so-called hopeless cases.

The clown is a metaphor for transcending limits. Jesus healed people, even rose from the dead. A clown does impossible feats, for example, makes water come out of a boutonniere or rides a bicycle across a tightrope. Christ can take problem people and transform them, like a rugged Peter who became the first preacher of the Christian church and won thousands to the gospel.

Hundreds of years ago the church expected clowns in worship services. They popped up from the congregation and mimed, did magic, mocked evil, performed in any of the ways clowns do, but in the interests of illustrating gospel truth to an illiterate age. The clowns' make-believe disarmed people and somehow opened the doors to belief. That's why some street preachers and church evangelists dress and perform as clowns today.

Clowns help us laugh at our helplessness. And once we laugh at it, we've admitted our need. Admitting is the price of admission into the kingdom. Jesus told us that when we become as little children we enter the kingdom of God. Buffoons have a way of clobbering artificiality, that ever-threatening blockade to God.

Well, no one wants mere entertainment in church, but we can thank God for clown ministry groups active in our time, for they remind us that letting down our barriers so God can come into our hearts, is a joyous, liberating affair.

Worship and the Right Side of the Brain

In a moment of inspired worship, Isaiah sings, "I will greatly rejoice in the Lord, my whole being shall exult in my God; for he has clothed me with the garments of salvation, he has covered me with the robe of righteousness, as a bridegroom decks himself with a garland, and as a bride adorns herself with her jewels" (Isaiah 61:10, NRSV). The joyous and pictorial quality of these words represents perfectly the dramatic nature of worship as the Bible understands it.

Worship is essentially a right brained activity — imaginative, picture producing, poetic and musical. The left brain engages in rational and cognitive activity. The right brain processes emotional and warm thoughts; the left hemisphere does the calculating and analysis.

We do not register surprise, then, when we learn that the laughter locus resides in the right brain. Research into victims who suffered right hemispherical brain damage showed them incapable of laughing at stories normal people found hilarious. While the left brain relates to some kinds of humor, the right brain often initiates laughter responses.

Serious material tends to reflect the left brain, and it communicates with corresponding difficulty. When, in fact, we need to say something heavy, especially in an audience made of people with mixed intellectual orientations, the best way to get through is first to do or say something imaginative. To get the emotions moving is to pave the runway into the left brain.

The Christian church has always intuited this principle. Thus Holy Communion reenacts the Last Supper; baptism relives the baptism of our Lord. Good sermons stimulate the imagination. Temple University studies revealed that only 7 percent of our communication is verbal; 38 percent is tonal; and 55 percent nonverbal (body language).

Wise worship leaders know that to get through to

45

the people they must resist cold abstraction, modify the linear, and process the logical. The painter's palette, the dramatist's movement and the humorist's stories must have their appropriate place. Although neither preachers nor parishioners need become frivolous, every human being craves genuine communication. That ministry comes naturally and fulfillingly when we sing in the spirit of the *Old Hundredth*: "Him serve with mirth, His praise forthtell."

4 How Did We Get So Sober?

The writer to the Hebrews, speaking of Jesus, talks about the "joy that was set before him" — that's why the Lord could endure the cross, despising its shame (Hebrews 12:2). But the cross seems to have taken precedence over the joy. Historically, Jesus has become the man of sorrows, acquainted with grief, more than the Son of God filled with the joy of His Father.

Yet in the Bible, both the Old and New Testaments, from beginning to end, from Genesis to Revelation, we hear a note of exuberance. Words for *joy* occur some 1,125 times in the Gospels alone!

Renan, the French writer, says Jesus "traversed Galilee in the midst of a continual feast. ... His entering a house was considered a joy and a blessing. He stopped in the villages and the large farms, where he was received with an eager hospitality. ... The mothers ... brought him their children in order that he might touch them. Women came to pour oil upon his head, and perfume on his feet."

The reason for the misleading goes back to Plato and Aristotle. These Greek men examined tragedy and comedy. They concluded that the human race comes across more honorably when seen through the eyes of tragic-drama rather than through the eyes of comic-drama. Comedy sees humanity less than it is; tragedy perceives it nobler than it is.

So when the theologians tackled Bible interpretation, they took Greek cues. They constructed a dark framework within which to work — man's depravity, the evilness of the world, and the answer in the crucifixion. The shove from Greek thinkers persists to this day. One of the chief theologians of the 20th century, Karl Barth, devotes but a single page to humor out of all the pages in his multi-volume *Dogmatics*. True, he discusses the resurrection, salvation, and a good many components of the Good News. Nonetheless, the little space given to humor symbolizes his tendency to look at the serious side of life before the lighter, upbeat side.

Ministers and theologians have often seen happy emotions as unworthy. Ambrose of Milan informed his clergy that "joking should be avoided even in small talk, so that some more serious topic is not made light of. ..."

But many people have avoided the church because they get the message that only depressives, at least terribly austere people, can really be good Christians!

Preaching and Scripture

No one can read Isaiah's famous words about the preacher without catching the prophet's own bounteous zest. "How beautiful upon the mountains are the feet of the messenger who announces peace, who brings good news, who announces salvation, who says to Zion, 'Your God reigns'" (Isaiah 52:7, NRSV). Nothing doleful there!

Nor in the Scriptures as a whole, does the mournful outrun the joyful in the story of the Hebrew nation, or the beginnings of the Christian community. God laughs in Psalms (2:4); God plays (Job 41:5); God likes us to laugh (Psalm 126, outset); and He promises laughter to His own (Luke 6:21b). Together these texts make a beautiful colleague:

> "He who sits in the heavens laughs. ..."
> "Will you play with him as with a bird ... ?"
> "Then our mouth was filled with laughter,
> and our tongue with shouts of joy. ..."

"Blessed are you that weep now, for you shall laugh." (Quotations from RSV.)

The Scriptures include games and playing, fables, and plays on words (some passages yield their deepest meaning only when the wordplay comes to light). Jesus' words include irony and some Old Testament passages project satire. We have a whole set of books called Wisdom Literature, which includes wit and riddle-like material. No one can read the book of Proverbs without smiling sooner or later.

In our day God blesses us with a growing number of preachers who have picked up on the joyful note in Scripture. They show themselves unafraid to have fun and to engage their listeners in a good laugh.

Lee F. Tuttle, in *Profiles of 20th Century Pulpit Giants*, treats 24 preachers and finds characteristics common to all, "but perhaps a sense of humor was the most unanimously a major [feature]." We do not need to look for the reason. These pulpit giants know Who stands in charge of the world, that God will win out in the end, that acceptance of our finitude brings us release, and that supposing we are little gods only makes us terribly ridiculous. They know that revolutionaries cannot laugh, but that liberators find delight everywhere they turn, and that genuine religion must come to balance in the lighter side of life.

Mirth, Balance, and Therapy

Laughter research, uncovering crucial data for information and improved living, signals mirth's capacity to restore balance to our lives. Balance in terms of mental outlook, perspective, physiology, faith and wholeness. St. Paul admonishes, "And let the peace of Christ rule in your hearts. ... And be thankful" (Colossians 3:15, RSV). In the very next verse, Paul's merry heart surfaces with the further admonition to "sing psalms and hymns and spiritual songs with thankfulness in your hearts to God."

We now know that laughter can reestablish peace, and when that happens our very physiologies change. For example, we have learned that kinetic energies, banked in the body's organisms, come to release in laughter, thus giving us motivation, drives and forward thrust. Mirth-response testing shows humor a factor in restoring and maintaining emotional well-being. Interestingly, the maladjusted persons in one test group, reacted negatively to the comic. Nervousness, resentment and general unhappiness resulted. Contrariwise, normal psyches enjoyed the delights of a funny story or joke, and their anxiety level lowered. Historically, psychiatrists have probably looked upon humor as an anxiety-reducing instrument.

Worship, private or public, ought to contribute to anxiety reduction. Robert Louis Stevenson, however, did not always experience that; in fact, he sometimes found going to church triggered discouragement.

Worship, by its very nature, ought to help us handle the incongruities of life. Reinhold Niebuhr is specific when he declares that both faith and humor help us cope with incompatibilities. Faith, Professor Niebuhr believed, deals with ultimate discordances, while humor helps us manage disparities in the here and now.

Bob W. Parrott, in *God's Sense of Humor*, has quite a bit to say about the incongruities of life. He points out that the recognition of them from the pulpit or on one's knees brings us to the understanding that God Himself takes control of our lives. When that knowledge sets in, faith operates. Wholesome humor rescues us from superiority, and superiority is the awful soberness that stifles liberation and spawns unbelief.

Do your own research. Notice the sense of contented adjustment that settles on a congregation after a good laugh. Comic relief can do that when people struggle to listen to a sermon, but the relief relates especially to the struggle of life itself. Observe your own feelings in private devotion when you see something in Scripture that tickles your mirth response into action. A happy heart refurbishes the mind with a sharpened view of life with all its experiences. Indeed, sometimes a whole new panorama stretches out before one's mind, bringing that fresh light and renewed strength that signifies balance.

7 Therapeutic Preaching

Surely Jesus had a twinkle in His eye when He referred to the pompous Pharisees who "preach, but do not practice." He denounces hypocrisy in Matthew 23, and the preaching-but-not-practicing bit gets at the center of it in all He said. One mark of some great preachers of history is humility that allows them to see themselves for what they are and laugh about it. That attitude generates a contagious spirit because people identify with imperfection. Only muffled laughs come in the presence of imperfection trying to come across as perfection.

Who the preacher is, then, becomes more important than what the preacher says. When one's authority has no power to rob one of true knowledge of self, and when the messenger can say by humor that he or she too is a sinner saved by grace, the preacher plugs into the audience.

Malcolm Muggeridge believes humor is the "disparity between human aspiration and human performance." The preacher who admits that will sooner or later be both a humorist and a therapist. Not that every time we can pull off comedy about the disparity between the ideal and the real; some things remain just plain heavy to bear. But after dealing with them head-on, a good laugh may initiate therapy. Jesus impresses us by His straightforward handling of the heavies in the story of the Prodigal, and after that He wisely injects relief with, "Let us make merry."

The spirit of Jesus' preaching is the spirit of the historic public prayer, the *Sursum corda*, "Lift up Your Hearts," often prayed responsively:

Lift up your hearts.
WE LIFT THEM UP UNTO THE LORD.

O Lord, open thou our eyes.
THAT WE MAY BEHOLD WONDROUS
THINGS OUT OF THY LAW.

O Lord, open thou our lips.
AND OUR MOUTH SHALL SHOW FORTH
THY PRAISE.

Praise ye the Lord.
THE LORD'S NAME BE PRAISED.

**Pastor Bob dealt with a disagreeable board member
in his own unique way.**

V

Gratitude

*"Gratitude is not only the greatest
of virtues, but the parent of all others."*

— Cicero

Have a Good Laugh

Sir Winston Churchill, standing at an upper level of the Houses of Parliament looking down on the walk below, saw Sir Stafford Cripps parading into the buildings. Sir Stafford carried himself with a great deal of pomp and ego. Sir Winston said in a voice loud enough for all around him to hear, "There, but for the grace of God, goes God."

The Attitude of Gratitude

The theme song of the book of Psalms is thanks. For example, Psalms 106:1: "Praise the Lord! O give thanks to the Lord, for he is good; for his steadfast love endures forever!" (NRSV)

1

America's first woman poet, Anne Bradstreet (1612-1672), daughter of a Massachusetts Bay Colony governor, also mother of eight, penned the following verse straight from her heart. It is a prayer of thanks, written when her husband returned home safely:

> What shall I render
> to thy Name,
> or how thy Praises speak;
> My thankes
> how shall I testefye?
> O Lord,
> thou know'st I'm weak.
> What could I more desire?
> But Thankfulness,
> even all my dayes,
> I humbly this Require.

Gratitude brings joy, often instantly. The reason for that is a spiritual law articulated by John Wesley: "Praise opens the door to more grace." And awareness of a fresh renewal of God's grace only generates more gratitude which in turn gives birth to multiplied joy.

2 Gratitude, Health, and Wholeness

Proverbs 16:24 reveals profound wisdom: "Pleasant words are like a honeycomb, sweetness to the soul and health to the body" (RSV). Gratefulness moves us to happy thoughts and language; that, in turn, we now know from biochemical studies, stimulates brain and body to physical health.

The reverse also obtains. That's why E. Stanley Jones lists the 12 apostles of ill health:

(1) Anger
(2) Resentments
(3) Fear
(4) Worry
(5) Desire to dominate
(6) Self-preoccupation

(7) Guilt

(8) Sexual impurity

(9) Jealousy

(10) A lack of creative activity

(11) Inferiorities

(12) A lack of love

The magic of a thankful spirit is that it has power to replace anger with love, resentment with happiness, fear with faith, worry with peace, the desire to dominate with the wish to play on a team, self-preoccupation with the needs of others, guilt with an open door to forgiveness, sexual impurity with honor and respect, jealousy with joy at another's success, lack of creativity with inspired productivity, inferiorities with dignity and a lack of love with an abundance of self-sharing.

The medical and mental health authorities say that the above twelvefold transformation spells both inner and outer well-being. Even for the one physically crippled, praise-filled lips bring wholeness and, in addition, uplift those in the presence of the physically challenged.

Amy Carmichael documents that: For two decades she administered an orphanage in India from her bed! When Billy Graham visited Dohnavur, locale of Miss Carmichael's home for destitute girls, he had to remove himself to the garden where he could weep in private. To read her life is to learn of the remarkable consistency of her joyful spirit whose wellspring was gratitude.

The genius of gratitude, unlike self-sympathy, is in the joy-producing product, wholeness.

A Key Clue to Happiness

"In the world you have tribulation," promises Jesus. Then He gives a higher promise, "but be of good cheer, I have overcome the world" (RSV). The first clause of that sentence from John 16:33 is simply a recognition of reality — life does have its battles. The last portion is admonition to joyful gratitude, a source of happiness. "How happy a

3

person is," John Miller observed, "depends upon the depth of his gratitude."

But how naive to believe that recognition of God's goodness is something one turns on or off like a water tap! A grateful attitude is, as someone wisely observed, "both delicate and mysterious. It can be crushed by the uplifting of a skeptical eyebrow; yet its psychology is hidden in the divine love." Do we find ourselves left, then, to the whim of circumstance? No indeed. The whole quest for a thankful heart, with its inevitable issuance in happiness, relates to developing a mind-set strong as an army with banners, sturdy as the Rock of Gibraltar. Christ calls us to establish gratitude as a lifestyle.

How do we establish that lifestyle? Three suggestions help answer that fundamental question.

(1) Ask for a grateful heart; ask simply and sincerely: *O Lord, that lends me life, Lend me a heart replete with thankfulness!* — Shakespeare

(2) Surrender your ego. Mark Twain got at this in his own ironical way. "If you pick up a starving dog and make him prosperous, he will not bite you; that is the principal difference between a dog and a man." Receiving gratefully requires humility; the practice of such selflessness develops strong spirituality.

(3) Decide to live gratefully whether you feel like it or not. The old James-Lange theory of psychology, that we feel like doing things after we start doing them, has a lot of merit to it. While that doesn't always work, it functions better than 90 percent of the time. So say you're grateful whether you want to or not, and you will usually feel grateful and happier because of your willing expression of thanks.

4 Remembering with Gratitude

The word "remember," in both Old and New Testaments, appears often and always with significant meaning. Psalm 98, for example, begins, "O sing to the Lord a new song, for he has done marvelous things. His right hand and his holy arm have gotten him victory." Then verse 3: "He has remembered his steadfast love and faithfulness to the house of Israel" (NRSV).

What strikes the Bible reader is the praise posture of the writers, the framework of gratefulness which holds the picture of the past. Even when events turn sour for the Israelites or Christians, the thrust of optimism maintains itself with persistence. Not that the Scripture avoids the realities of the past; escapism never issues in joy and never characterizes the stance of the Bible writers.

What we have in Holy Writ is the unveiling of a secret to handling memories, personal and social. The secret is this, gratitude not only makes possible living with the past but seeing it in perspective. We can live with anything as long as we know God brings purpose to it. Nor must we have all details in mind; even when we can not know the details, we live in the faith that God uses all.

Romans 8:28 promises that all things work together for good to those who love God; that is a law of life. God wastes nothing. He creates out of the chaotic, recreates out of suffering, and often orders our affairs better than ever, as in the case of Job.

Individuals who have experienced healing for bad memories find that when gratitude reigns, the past takes on a new sweep of understanding and peace follows. The process of becoming self-aware and openly honest may issue at first in painful catharsis. But it is catharsis. Anger turns to constructive uses, love takes over the will, and hope replaces hate. Gratitude is the dynamic that makes therapy reality. Cicero spoke insightfully, "Gratitude is not only the greatest of virtues, but the parent of all others."

We must take the initiative in gratitude. Said Charles E. Jefferson, the American preacher, "Gratitude is born in hearts that take time to count up past mercies." That may not prove as difficult as it first appears, for psychologists have discovered that we tend to remember good experiences and forget the bad. So when we suffer some little injustice we'd best laugh it off, and let it rest in God's kind hand, knowing He works for our good. That's a sure way to live in joy instead of bitterness, and is the real documentation for memory healing.

5 Giving Thanks Always

St. Paul tells us over and again in Philippians to give thanks in every circumstance.

Bill Stidger, that unusual preacher and teacher of preachers, sat about with friends one Thanksgiving day during the Great Depression. The grumbling that emerged finally prompted someone to suggest a turn of conversation to a positive direction. After all, Christians should express affirmation and appreciation! And how about starting with those who had done them good?

Bill thought of Mrs. Wendt, his high school teacher who introduced him to Tennyson, Browning and other poets. The upshot: he took pen in hand and wrote Mrs. Wendt a thank you note. The response he got from the lady, now very old and in a rest home, gratified him so much that he began sending appreciation letters to other folks. In fact, he determined to make November his annual write-thank-you-notes month.

He remembered, for example, how Mrs. McDowell, wife of Bishop William F. McDowell, had showed kindness to him before a speaking engagement. "Seeing that I was tired out," remembers Bill Stidger, "Mrs. McDowell put me to bed to rest, and I was so grateful for that motherly thoughtfulness that I never forgot it." Yet, he admitted he had never once said thank you. But by the time he got around to sending a letter, Mrs. McDowell had died. So he wrote the bishop, rehearsing the memory in some detail. Dr. Stidger received a most touching response in which Bishop McDowell confessed that tears came to his eyes. He explained that he called out his wife's name and started to show her Will's letter; he had forgotten for the moment that she had gone. Will, as the bishop called his younger friend, would never know how the letter "has warmed my spirit. I have been walking in the glow of it all day long."

That letter typified over 500 responses Professor Stidger got over a ten year period.

St. Paul told us to give thanks in any and all circumstances, even to take the initiative in expressing gratitude. I, for one, want to live like Paul and Bill Stidger. God, grant me the grace of expressed gratitude.

The Prayer That Brings Joy

St. Paul, in the crucible of his suffering, cries out from his prison cell with words that would make one think he wrote from a hotel room overlooking the Tiber River. He announced, "Have no anxiety about anything, but in everything by prayer and supplication with thanksgiving let your requests be made known to God." As if that weren't enough joyful expression, he adds, "And the peace of God, which passes all understanding, will keep your hearts and your minds in Christ Jesus" (Philippians 4:6-7, RSV).

"A single grateful thought toward heaven," said a sensitive soul, "is the most complete prayer." Gratitude opens God's heart and lets answers to prayer flow. Perhaps God's feelings identify rather much with ours; after all, we feel good and generous when someone expresses genuine appreciation to us. If "gratitude is the homage of the heart, rendered to God for his goodness," as Nathaniel Parker Willis said, then God's heart responds to it, and He unleashes heaven's blessings in a great Niagara of returning love.

In my work as a minister and counselor, I have noticed that those who make thankfulness the style of their lives, get answers to their prayers. Even answers hard to come by. I have also observed the reverse, that those who complain miss the answers God desires to give, and their problems multiply. Charles Spurgeon, a long time ago, put this truth in succinct language: "When we bless God for mercies we prolong them. When we bless Him for miseries we usually end them."

One other facet of this divine reality: We help God with His work when we share the best. That's why Edwin Percy Whipple observed, "God is glorified, not by our groans, but by our thanksgivings." An American preacher instructing other American preachers, warned that to send people away from church on flat tires is a sin. By the same token, Christians wrong people when they spread negativity, but spreading good news is as right as rain. Then others, too, will have the door opened to the answered prayer that brings joy.

7 The Witness of Gratitude

St. Paul, closing Philippians, makes an astonishing statement, "All the saints greet you, especially those of Caesar's household" (4:22, RSV). Imagine! Saints in Caesar's household.

Now, how in the world did Paul succeed in getting converts in this tightly closed pagan in-group? Surely the texture and context of the whole book of Philippians gives us the answer. Throughout the letter, Paul praises God; even when he has hard words to write, he couches them in a thankful tone. The poor man had every reason to complain, but he did not. In point of fact, the student of the letter to the Philippian church will search in vain even to discover where Paul suffered imprisonment. Rome? Caeserea? Ephesus? Scholars suggest all three places, but we cannot know.

Gratitude like that makes people ask probing questions. What causes that lifestyle? Where does it come from? What sustains the suffering man's joy? No doubt Paul heard questions like these from Caesar's servants. And surely he had ready answers. When, at last, the emperor's workers saw the transparency of their prisoner, saw him not as a fake, they wanted the same power in their own lives. With that opening into their hearts, Paul led them to Christ.

The evangelism of the world is our biggest calling. Our next largest challenge is to create the evangelists to do the job. The first mark, the most telling characteristic required, is the attitude of gratitude.

Read the first church history book, the Acts of the Apostles, and try to come to a definition of Christian witness. After study and thought you will suggest such words as *radiance, contagion, joy*. To this day that's what brings people to the feet of Christ. And that's what keeps people coming in a steady flow to the gospel.

We noticed in an earlier reading segment that the final word of the Acts of the Apostles is *unhindered*. Nothing stops the witness of glad gratitude.

"Check and see if Mrs. Belcher is on the same page
as the rest of us."

VI

Faith and the Joyous Spirit

"My most cherished possession
I wish I could leave you
is my faith in Jesus Christ,
for with Him and nothing else
you can be happy,
but without Him and with all else
you'll never be happy."

— Patrick Henry

Have a Good Laugh

Of the many funny epitaphs, this one strikes us as especially humorous because of its hilarious rhyming. It comes from England.

Here under this sod and under these trees
Is buried the body of Solomon Pease.
But here in this hole lies only his pod
His soul is shelled out and gone to God.

1 The Joyous Liberation of Faith

Jesus declared that, "You will know the truth, and the truth will make you free" (John 8:32, RSV). Faith and humor live close to one another; they throw up the blinds of the soul to see truth, which makes us free and joyous. Truth is our homeland, the soul's native soil, and God made us for truth, our natural place of residence.

Authentic faith lifts restraints. It lets us out of the jail we erect for ourselves and breaks the prison bars strengthened by society. Faith purifies perspectives on life and lets in love. A good laugh encourages the clear, clean mind and reminds us that love, not hate, makes life work. Faith integrates life; in moments of liberated laughter we sense that integration. Faith brings heaven close; laughter is like an angel opening earth to heaven. Faith drops unnecessary fights and puts us in the right battle. Laughter restores the mind to perceive, and the heart to serve God's army. Faith, like gravity, pulls us to the center; laughter supports that pull and helps us see the center with renewed clarity. It does more. It expands our view of life, and that is the genius of its liberating power.

Faith and humor are musts for fruitful living. With them life unfolds its mysterious complexity in portions we can handle. "Humor is essential to any smoothly functioning system of interaction," said a wise man, it is indispensable "to any healthy person, and to any viable group. Humor is, in the last analysis, no joke." One reason is this, humor oils the wheels of life's machinery, and this liberation lets God build in us a framework of faith that makes possible saying what needs saying and doing what needs doing.

Robin Williams believes that "comedy is acting out optimism." Optimism is joyous faith alive. It takes off the clothes of fear and redresses us in the garb of hope. It melts the tension of frozen anxiety, restores spontaneity, and sees the good in whatever happens.

Paul observed that, "Where the Spirit of the Lord is,

there is freedom" (2 Corinthians 3:17, RSV). Have you noticed that laughter in a Christian setting not only encourages faith but relates closely to the Spirit of God?

Laughter Builds Faith

The writer of Psalm 96 sings, "Let the heavens be glad, and let the earth rejoice; let the sea roar, and all that fills it; let the field exult, and everything in it!" (verses 11-12a, RSV). The psalmist goes on in that vein using the joy of nature to model a happy spirit. Earlier in that Psalm, the writer tells us joyous song is a good vehicle for witnessing to other nations about the glory of God.

Joy and laughter communicate faith, and that happens when we use humor to build up others. To tear down by going for the jugular instead of the jocular vein, stops faith before it gets to its goal. But wholesome laughter becomes a means of self-identification; helps it build a sound self-image; it alters moods; it serves like a cartoon by getting us to have fun with ourselves; it projects empathy and establishes rapport; and it turns negativity into positivity.

Just at that last point, the matter of positivity, I once asked a college president the secret of his optimism. He gave me three ideas I cannot forget: (1) Decide to be positive; (2) Be positive; (3) Remember that if you lose your optimism, you lose your leadership. Every knowing Christian wants to lead others into positive faith. Whether one is a college president or an unsung Christian helping others in the daily flow of life, these three guidelines give us a clue for working with God in the grand business of propagating the faith.

Add laughter to the college president's three points, and you've got a winning combination! That president does possess a marvelous sense of humor. For decades it has served to strengthen his faith which consistently issues in positive leadership and influence. Ask anyone who knows him, and you will hear something like this,

"Just to be around him makes you stronger."

The Contagion of Humor and Faith

In the Gospels, Jesus heals person after person. The healings can take place because Jesus stimulates faith. Of the woman healed in Matthew 9, Jesus says, "Take heart, daughter; your faith has made you well" (v. 22, NRSV).

The reverse can take place. Sneering has power to rob people of faith, which explains why Jesus ordered scoffers out of the room where he would bring a girl to life. The scoffers "laughed at" Jesus (Matthew 9:24). Destructive laughter, Jesus knew, destroys faith.

But faith and humor, once married, produce a contagious spirit that has great power for creating good. Thus, when health care professionals encourage pleasantries, therapy gets a boost. More good news is that doctors, nurses, ministers, anybody in the health and wholeness fields, find the nurture of laughter easier in this age of openness. Professionals have historically created an aura rather too solemn and austere to engage in very much humor.

A whole new movement in the medical profession — gallows humor — sees mirth designed to cope with death and the constant round of challenges in operating theater and hospital room. One doctor put it this way, "Our humor is a protective device. If we were to talk seriously all the time and act like a bunch of Sir Galahads ... we just couldn't take all this." Sometimes patients open themselves enough to engage in gallows humor with the health professionals. That puts everybody at ease and assists in activating faith. One researcher even discovered that humor can serve well as a teaching device whereby seasoned doctors, while instructing novices, can help soften the blows of tragedy, initial clinical shock, and the grim realities of suffering.

The medical community now explores the cultivation of humor as a tool of therapy. H. Mindness did a work entitled, *Humor and Laughter: Theory, Research, and Applications*. He investigated the uses and abuses of humor in psychotherapy. Another scholar, Vera M. Robinson, did a volume on humor in nursing, *Behavioral Concepts and Nursing Intervention*, and also produced *Humor and the Health Professions*.

You will notice that Jesus always encouraged faith. He knew its power. Conversely, he dealt forthrightly with any who endangered faith. Well-used pleasantries can put us on Jesus' team and make faith delightfully contagious.

Humor, Faith, and Healing

4

Hebrews 11:1 introduces the classic faith chapter with these words, "Now faith is the assurance of things hoped for, the conviction of things not seen" (NRSV). The assumption of the entire chapter is that faith develops with cultivation. No, one cannot manufacture it, for faith is a gift. It is like the body. We ourselves did not make it — God did. We must cultivate a good physiology if we expect to stay healthy and whole.

One way to keep faith sound is to laugh. In turn, humor becomes the vehicle of passing health on to the body. The philosopher Kant said in 1790, long before modern research on fitness and jocularity, that jokes nurture the "vital bodily processes" and generate a "favorable influence on health."

We could say the same of psychological well-being. Today we find increasing documentation that humor prevents or helps cure depression. In fact, the whole range of emotions seems touched by laughter. Thus Vera M. Robinson, reporting in Volume II of the *Handbook of Humor Research*, says this: "Certainly, there has been much support for the emotionally therapeutic value of humor as an adaptive, coping behavior, as a catharsis for and relief of tension, as a defense against depression, as a sign of emotional maturity, and as a survival mechanism."

When we feel good, faith comes easier; when we encourage faith, we feel better. Herein lies enough reason to release ourselves to laughter, which in turn can release us to fresh faith. F.W. Fry discovered that emotional catharsis parallels physiological response when laughter sets in. He observes that laughter compares to physical exercise, what with oxygen exchange, increase of muscular activity, and the stimulation of the cardiovascular and sympathetic nervous systems, even blood pressure reduces to a healthier level. Fry says laughter plays its role in preventing heart disease, cerebral vascular accidents, cancer and other problems.

Researcher after researcher has come up with the good effects of mirth on both body and psyche. The values range from tension reduction to left-brain right-brain stimulus. The latter, counselors may use someday in psychotherapy because when the two hemispheres function adequately, patients have a better chance to see both the logical and abstract phases of their problem.

Faith, healing and laughter go together. Laughter plays its role by maintaining and enriching spontaneous belief that can in turn bring welcome healing.

5 Restoring Sanity

After Jesus had identified Himself, John comments that, "As he [Jesus] spoke thus, many believed in him" (John 8:30, RSV). Jesus modeled life and thought at the highest and sanest level. His joy, enthusiasm, belief in people and capacity to face reality (sometimes with humor), all become our criteria for right-mindedness.

When Will Rogers advised, "We are all here for a spell. Get all the good laughs you can," he struck a chord in all of us, the chord that firms up strong, stable thinking. Norman Cousins talks about "that apothecary inside you," by which he means that humor is medicine. When the medicine works, muddled thinking clears like a stirred stream after sediment settles.

Clarity of mind and active faith are bedfellows, for though the Christian knows the fixed substratum of faith no matter how he or she feels, when the sediment settles, faith's power revitalizes itself. In a sense, faith is sanity. A faith-oriented life functions well on all levels. If humor aids in restoring the balance that is sanity, faith binds life in an integrated working whole.

"Stress" and "burnout" have become everyday words in our fast-paced world. Humor has a way of clearing the psyche so we can see to wash the decks. But it goes further. A Tel Aviv University researcher demonstrated that laughter enhances both learning and creativity. He also learned laughter maximizes memory. Evidently a merry heart activates the brain and achieves balance and strength.

Faith and Comedy

Jesus encouraged us with His familiar words, "In the world you have tribulation; but be of good cheer, I have overcome the world" (John 16:33, RSV).

Comedians help us to press the cheer key of the computer. They help us come at life with fresh perspective and new faith. Bill Cosby can show us the fun in family problems; Bob Hope helps us poke fun at ourselves; Art Buchwald rescues us from taking the government too seriously. When we can look at others, and especially ourselves, without a poker face, we've found a grand secret of liberation and joy. The awful gravity with which we go after success, and the equal pensiveness that accompanies our failures — well, we need to let the air out of those pompous balloons.

Laughter restores clearheaded thinking. That frame of mind brings the Christian back to a faith stance. Without that change, we soon move from seriousness to self-pity, and faith falters just there. Put positively, comedy buoys faith.

Meditative reflection has its place in problem solving and faith building. Solutions usually come with hard thinking. But our reflective times must break loose from undue heaviness of spirit. Sometimes, in fact, we must set aside decision making until emotions stabilize. In any event, thinking marked by active faith yields genuine possibilities.

The achieving of that possibility posture is crucial. A walk in the woods may bring it; a phone conversation with an inspiring friend may restore it; or a good meal may initiate it. But the astonishing quality of humor is that more often than not, it brings us right back to the place where faith can dominate us, and where, therefore, God can see us meet challenges with poise and success.

7 The Rest of Faith

The classic passage in Isaiah 30:15 (RSV) summarizes the soul's rest found in authentic faith: "For thus said the Lord God, the Holy One of Israel, 'In returning and rest you shall be saved; in quietness and in trust shall be your strength.'"

One of the great but not often heard hymns of the last century, came from the knowing pen of Lidie H. Edmunds:

> My faith has found a resting place,
> Not in device nor creed;
> I trust the Everliving One,
> His wounds for me shall plead.

REFRAIN:
> I need no other argument,
> I need no other plea,
> It is enough that Jesus died,
> And that he died for me.

The second verse unfolds the security of wholeness in Christ:

> Enough for me that Jesus saves,
> This ends my fear and doubt;

A sinful soul I come to him,
He'll never cast me out.

The final stanza knows the faith that heals:
My great physician heals the sick,
The lost he came to save;
For me his precious blood he shed,
For me his life he gave.

Oswald Chambers caught the point at which security becomes real and joy authentic, "The joy that Jesus gives is the result of our disposition being at one with his own disposition." Chambers suffered an attack of ill health, died prematurely, but knew the "rest of faith" and, therefore, Christian joy. He learned that trying to find his security in circumstances ends in a *cul-de-sac*; he knew the reality of Isaiah 30:15.

Modern psychotherapy since Carl Jung has known about and encouraged active, secure faith. Jung's famous statement about people who find faith getting well, and those who avoid a working faith staying sick — that truth sticks with us. Christians take Jung a step further to say that in Jesus we find unshakable security and, therefore, that wellness which spells unshakable joy in the depths of the personality.

The very name *Jesus* means wholeness, and wholeness is another name for rest which is a significant dynamic of joy.

Emily felt God calling Earl to the altar.

VII

Love, Laughter and Life

*"In our life there is a single color,
as on an artist's palette,
which provides the meaning
of life. It is the color of love."*

— Marc Chagall

Have a Good Laugh

The pastor announced that he would do a series of sermons on "Christian Perfection."

"Has anyone in the congregation achieved perfection?" he asked. A little man stood up under the balcony. The amazed pastor asked, "Oh, Mr. Jones, have you achieved the perfect state?"

"No," he replied. "I'm standing for my wife's first husband."

The Love Environment

Interesting for its textual variables, 1 John 1:4 may read, "And we are writing this that our joy may be complete," or "... that your joy may be complete." The reason some manuscripts read *your* and some *our* may be far more profound than a mere slip of the pen by ancient copyists. The "our" may relate to the atmosphere of fellowship, to the sheer togetherness and free exchange characteristic of the early Christians. After all, love procreates love, and when one group extends joy, the very extenders receive joy in their own spirits.

This suggests the principle behind Mother Teresa's requirement that the corridors and rooms of her healing homes must fill with laughter. Can you imagine? Laughter among the deprived, depressed and distraught? How wise! She knows full well that in a joyful atmosphere, hope, health and healing take on new impetus. Even the dying capture fresh vision in a happy place.

Leo Buscaglia, in his best-selling *Loving Each Other*, makes this sound statement, "A bond of love is easy to find in an environment of joy." He goes on, "When we laugh together we bypass reason and logic, as the clown does. We speak a universal language. We feel closer to one another." Such an atmosphere!

People of all ages have learned, sometimes from rugged trial and error, that glad sharing creates *koinonia*; whereas, sad talking develops a counterproductive yield. Who hasn't watched tensions dissolve in the presence of love, joy, and humor?

Love Is A Decision and So Is Joy

When Jesus said, "Be perfect even as your father in heaven ... ," He gave us an invitation to fulfillment.

Abraham Lincoln declared that, "Most folks are about as happy as they make up their minds to be." One of the best-selling books on depression develops the thesis that *Happiness Is a Choice*. While some critics assess the book as simplistic, its theme expresses enough truth, as Lincoln's dictum. This makes us pause for thought.

But what about joy? For the Christian, the presence of Christ, which is joy, brings stability through the experiences of life ... like a wheel, the rim goes over bumpy turf (life's disappointments) but the hub (joy) remains firm. Then comes the crunch. We can allow the hurts of life to inject their poison against the very joy God gives in His Son, Jesus Christ. We have all seen supposedly established Christians leave the Way, or more subtly, keep going to church while nursing anger.

Joy is like love for one's spouse. To maintain it one must make a daily decision ... analogous to Paul's spirit when he said he died daily; he gave up his "right" to self-sympathy and all the negation that implies.

Itzhak Perlman, though crippled by polio, is a contented man. Asked why, he says he made a decision years ago to look for the happy elements in life. He goes on to say others have made the opposite choice, to look for the unpleasant in the world.

Clearly Jesus' "Be perfect" implies our ability to decide. The word *perfect* means complete, whole ... in everyday language, joyful, happy. It is a chief secret of personal fulfillment.

Loving Yourself

We often hear with both ears, "Love your neighbor," but frequently listen with only one ear to those two important words, "as yourself." Jesus expects us to take seriously both parts of the command. Indeed, He knows, as does modern psychology, that we are projective persons — when we love others truly, we love ourselves too; when we enjoy self-esteem, we respect others also.

Laughing at ourselves means disarming our perfectionism. As the authors of *Happiness Is a Choice* say about overcoming depression, "Laughter relaxes us as almost nothing else can. Many individuals improve as soon as they learn no one is perfect (not even they) and as they begin to laugh at their own perfectionistic demands or other shortcomings."

Actually, we become therapists when we engage ourselves and others in laughter. Luciano de Crescenzo said, "We are each of us angels with only one wing. And we can only fly embracing each other." Antisocial persons tend to become depressed; whereas, those who are wholesomely social send out signals of joy and love, and appreciate help in flying. Flying makes us feel good about ourselves and about associating with others.

Miles of research documents the simple truth that those who love can receive love. Humor not only oils the skids for love, it is a vehicle of mutual attraction. In an atmosphere of healthy feedback, we love ourselves naturally and easily.

Part of the trick lies in the friends we choose. An ambiance of easy give-and-take works better than liquor for loosening tongues, creating laughter and the kind of socializing that makes us feel comfortably joyous. Angry, grouchy people manufacture a different set of vibrations. Getting "in" with the happy people early in life carries far-reaching implications for the development of that mental health which is self-respect.

The implications extend to every phase of existence. Leo Buscaglia observes that, "When we feel joyful, euphoric, happy, we are more open to life, more capable of seeing things clearly and handling daily tensions." In other words, we relate normally to every dimension — things, persons, God and of course ourselves. What other lifestyle can affirm and help generate real self-love and its offspring, joy?

Love One Another

First John, which uses the word *love* nearly 50 times, gives us the test of wholeness, "We know that we have passed out of death into life, because we love the brethren." When Jesus told us to love one another as He loves us, He shared the secret of joy-filled living.

The love-one-another theme has captured a good many minds. Commented the ancient writer, Statius Caecilius, "They [the Christians] know one another by secret marks and signs, and they love one another almost before they know one another."

The modern writer Harry Stack Sullivan, says that, "When the satisfaction or security of another person becomes as important to one as one's own, then a state of love exists."

Human behavior research tells us the secret of happiness, personal security and even success, is the capacity to relate to others with love and trust. Contrariwise, insecurities, fears, ineptitudes, even mental disease, come by harboring interpersonal feelings that foster anger and mistrust.

One of the practical ways to develop loving rather than negative relationships is simply taking the initiative to do acts of kindness for people. We have this principle modeled in recent findings from dental research. In the *Journal of the American Dental Association*, K. Seyrek, D.D.S. and Norman Corah, Ph.D., from Buffalo's State University of New York Dental School, tell of getting patients to play video games and watch comedy. Those who did one or the other during dental procedures suffered less pain than those who simply listened to audio tapes of comedy routines. Why? Distraction, says Dr. Corah. *Prevention Magazine*, reviewing the research, reports the conclusion, "Both the video game and the comedy film were better at helping patients transfer their attention to something other than what the dentist was doing."

This experiment illustrates all over again the propensity of the scientific community toward helping (loving) people. Concrete ways of loving one another take on perspective for Christians when evangelist David Wilkerson says, "Love is not only something you feel. It's something you do." That's why Norman Vincent Peale observed, "Just having enough love in your heart for people to get out there and help them, you will experience exquisite joy and live with enthusiasm and joyous excitement."

In a remarkable book, *Love Is My Meaning*, the foreword by H.M. Queen Elizabeth the Queen Mother, we read a lovely passage on the relationship of prayer to helping and loving others. Prayers not only get us into the heart of God, says the writer; they also put us into contact with the need of the world. "It is only as we share God's love and care, however feebly, that we can penetrate beneath the surface in meeting and helping others in their deepest needs. ..." When we do that, joy inevitably results.

5 The Joy of Loving Your Spouse

The Bible says a great deal about husbands and wives. For example, Ephesians 5, where we read, "Wives, be subject to your husbands as you are to the Lord" (v. 22), and "husbands should love their wives as they do their own bodies" (v. 28, NRSV). Profound happiness awaits couples who follow those prescriptions.

The marriage at Cana, at which Jesus performed his first miracle, is an interpretive take off center for New Testament marriage-and-family teaching.

The undertone of the Cana story is joy. Marriage is a happy realization. Jesus says something more — it's OK to be happy, to laugh and to have fun. Comedians, clowns and town humorists have their legitimate place, but we can make our own fun. Jesus encouraged the self-generating joy of which all love is an expression.

Current studies imply that a pleasant atmosphere contributes to better interpersonal relationships, including a spirit that enhances home life. Erma Bombeck, in an interview for *Book Review Digest*, listened with rapt interest to the question, What does humor really accomplish? She answered with the word *everything* and then added what it could do for marriage. Even when a couple gets to arguing and sees their marriage falling apart, if that couple will restore humor, they will stop their gloomy mood and say, "Hey, we're going to be all right." Aunt Erma's wisdom punches holes in our unrelenting preoccupation with problems, a frame of mind that always spawns black thoughts and dismal solutions.

Add an eleventh commandment to your value system, habitually I will see the delight of life and pass that on to my spouse.

I once asked a university president how he kept going. His immediate answer, "Humor." Surely Lincoln Steffens answered in similar context when he declared, "The only thing worth having in an earthly existence is a sense of humor."

When a marriage gets tough, the tough get it going again with life-changing mirth.

Love Life and Enjoy It!

St. Paul quotes Isaiah in 1 Corinthians 2:9 (NRSV), "What no eye has seen, nor ear heard, nor the human heart conceived, what God has prepared for those who love him." You cannot begin to calculate the possibilities of life in Christ. And what releases those possibilities? God Himself, for He brings love and joy, the structural steel for building Life Abundant.

The prayer of faith believes that; it pierces the hard shell of unbelief. Unbelief? Yes, that cultural conditioning against happiness. Have you noticed that society tells us we should not expect to live joyfully? That if we do experience happiness, then we will surely suffer some reverse?

Couple that underlying feeling tone with our hesitancy to laugh. Someone told me at a book club meeting one evening, after a number of us had occupied ourselves in hearty laughter over a 10 or 15 minute period, that I really must control my mirthful instincts because, "Aren't you a seminary professor?"

Our minds, fed on the basic assumption of that

question, move into reverse gear when we might enjoy uproarious laughter. Drunks may laugh hilariously, clowns may release their inhibitions, but to come across as sane and serious about life, we must keep our dignity. What an implied definition of dignity!

God expects nature's spontaneity to come out. We all have a bit of clown in us, some more than others, but we all have it. When we squelch the inner clown, we set up conflicts. We attempt to resolve them by searching outwardly, supposing we will locate life "out there" somewhere.

That mistake Soren Kierkegaard saw clearly. The famous Dane showed the positive outworking of his principle. When, he observed, a person who "is always turned toward the outside, thinking that his happiness lies outside himself, finally turns inward and discovers that the source is within him" — when that happens, life can come to realization.

Read the New Testament and see that life comes with Christ. He is Life and He is Joy. No inhibitions in Him, yet, dignity flowers to its best bloom. How often He socialized with Mary, Martha and Lazarus! He walked country roads admiring the flowers. He also exposed the legalism of stiff and starchy persons. "Once we realize that Christ was not always engaged in pious talk," says Elton Trueblood in *The Humor of Christ*, "we have made an enormous step on the road to understanding." Trueblood talks about "freeing the gospel from the excessive sobriety." When we do that, we make progress freeing ourselves to love life and engage in its intended joys.

How to Restore Love of Life

"Laziness brings on deep sleep," says Proverbs 19:15 (NRSV). That sleep robs life of its buoyant cheer.

In the Middle Ages, the Second Deadly sin — the one we know as sloth — writers called *accidie*. Chaucer refers to "The synne of Accidie." The word doesn't even appear in today's unabridged Webster's, but we know the phenomenon well.

Accidie dictates deep dislike for one's environment. Like the nurse who said of her workplace, "I'm fed up with every nook and cranny." Her world had become dullsville; even the desert would look better! She went nowhere fast, and thought people didn't like her very much. She just wanted to stop work, to relieve herself of concentrating on anything. Her attempts at conversation ended in a downbeat mood.

The French call this mood *ennui*, what we term boredom. Mind you, not mere laziness; in our workaholic age we need do-nothing periods. Perhaps the nurse worked rather too continuously, without hobbies and reading, or any diversion to relax her. Whatever the cause of *ennui*, she found herself devoid of that flow of love which yields exhilaration.

How do we go about recovering from accidie, from this sloth that cheats us of life?

(1)   Since accidie is really a loss of faith in life, tackle faith-building head on. Confess your "deep sleep" and confess it with honesty. You're already on second base when you do that much. Then, decide for God, others and yourself all over again. Attitude is always a choice. Never mind how you feel at the moment; settle for life with a positive thrust. Then watch faith grow.

(2)   Since accidie also relates to others, clear the decks for wholesome relationships. Almost without exception, accidie emerges from some negative interpersonal experience ... like a communication breakdown between you and a family member or a colleague at work. Give your people problems to God; then observe mood change for the better. If you must apologize to someone, do it.

(3)   Since accidie relates to your life goals, renew your dreams. Never mind the broken hopes; all that's history. Oil your dream machine with up-to-date purposes for living. Determine to live grandly, largely, to the fullest; then know the love of life that is joy.

VIII

Slaying Dragons with the Weapon of Joy

*"... the dragon shalt thou tread
under thy feet."*
— Book of Common Prayer

*"Saint George, that swinged the dragon,
and e're since
Sits on his horseback
at mine hostess' door."*
— Shakespeare

*"If you would rule the world quietly,
You must keep it amused."*
— Emerson

Have a Good Laugh

I love finding mirthful stories. One I discovered in the delightful book, *Amusing Grace*, by King Duncan and Angela Akers. I tell it in my own words.

A gentleman, suffering from a splitting headache, went to the doctor. The nurse told him to go to the examining room and remove his clothes.

"Why should I do that?" he queried. "I only have a headache."

"Go into the room and remove your clothes," she said firmly.

His clothes off, he noticed another undressed gentleman in the examining room. Smiling a bit self-consciously, he commented, "How silly to take your clothes off just for a headache."

"You think that an inconvenience!" came the reply. "I came just to read the meter!"

1 Anger, Wrath, and Joyous Prayer

In Ephesians 4:31, St. Paul cries out against "bitterness and wrath and anger and wrangling and slander" (NRSV). *Put them away!* he admonishes. In their place, he says in verse 32, substitute kindness and forgiveness. In Colossians 3, he exhorts us to "get rid of ... anger, wrath, malice, slander, and abusive language" and to clothe "yourselves with the new self, which is being renewed in knowledge according to the image of its creator" (verses 8 and 10, NRSV).

Paul places anger and wrath side by side to encompass some detrimental emotions. *Wrath* literally means to boil or flame up, as when you put gasoline on green tree cuttings. On the other hand, the word *anger* means continuous, even habitual, long-lived vexation. Paul's clear message: do something about both wrath and anger.

Ancient Greeks likened the wrath that flames up to burning straw, it happens all at once. So boiling wrath is a fire in a Kansas wheat field. Paul announces that such flaming rage is sin, a sin of the flesh (Galatians 5:16-21).

Long-standing anger, like doubt, is a hindrance to prayer (1 Timothy 2:8). A remarkable devotional volume,

God Calling, entitles the November first reading, "Prayer of Joy." It begins, "Prayer can be like incense, rising ever higher and higher, or it can be like a low earth-mist clinging to the ground, never once soaring." Lifestyle anger hinders prayer. "But the prayer of real faith is the prayer of Joy, that sees and knows the heart of Love, it rises to greet, and that is so sure of a glad response."

The book of James (1:19-20) tells us to stay away from anger (long-range) because God's righteousness has a hard time thriving in that vengeful atmosphere. Jesus warns that this kind of anger erupts in calling people names and insults; such behavior in turn prompts the judgment of God (Matthew 5:22) and does not encourage a glad spirit.

A proverb from the Iglulik Eskimos reminds us that, "Evil prevails where laughter is not known."

Joy and Some Research Findings

Psalms 65 and 66, in *Today's English Version*, come at life with joy as a basic assumption. Hear, for example, Psalms 65:12-13, "The pastures are filled with flocks; the hillsides are full of joy. The fields are covered with sheep; the valleys are full of wheat. Everything shouts and sings for joy." The outset of Psalm 66 picks up the same motif, "Praise God with shouts of joy, all people! Sing to the glory of his name; offer him glorious praise! Say to God, 'How wonderful are the things you do! Your power is so great that your enemies bow down in fear before you.'"

We now know from research that this joyful attitude generates good health, staves off oncoming illness, and provides coping strength to get goals achieved. Take, for example, the research findings recorded in *USA Today*, "Personality affects immune cell strength, which influences whether people become sick or not. ..." The findings, reported to an American Psychological Association meeting in Los Angeles, strike us at once as newsworthy and reflect a fundamental posture of Scripture.

85

"Tests on the immune system show that it's not stress," the report goes on "but our way of responding to it that triggers illness." The psalmist might have groused about the hard work of farming and the reverses nature brings; instead, he praises God for His role in productivity.

For research, 190 medical students submitted to testing. Those who looked gloomily on exam time suffered less immunity and more illness; those who saw the experience as challenge rather than threat, heightened their immune ability.

A five year study of some 55 Three Mile Island residents (near Harrisburg, PA), showed that the presence of threat lowered physical immune capacity and increased stress-linked hormones. In other words, the threat seemed to be a greater deterrent to health than the actual nuclear accident.

Still another research reported in the *USA Today* article relates to herpes patients. Those depressed wrestle with "significantly more recurrences of the disease" than the optimistic. They also show lower immune cell function than the positive-minded people and the 36 patients studied demonstrated a decline in immune cell stamina just prior to a herpes attack.

Entertaining the dragon of fear may result in illness or failure; that in turn, rears the head of another dragon, anger. Contrariwise, joy, optimism and positivity spell faith which in turn writes itself in our minds and our very body chemistry.

Three Dragons and Money

Jesus admonished us to develop treasure in heaven, and said that earthbound riches have a way of yielding disappointment. Eternal investments bring joy.

On the surface, Jesus' statement in Matthew 6:19-21, about laying up treasures in heaven instead of earth, looks incongruous, yet we know greed's results. As William Barclay says, "The strange thing about the sin of avarice and the desire for money is that we think about it, and when we see what it means we wonder how anyone could be such a fool as to be guilty of it!" But everyone wants to get rich, and even morally responsible people would like to see if they can acquire wealth while avoiding the pitfalls.

Money has, through the centuries, given rise to a great deal of joke telling. We attempt to cope with life's inconformabilities by laughter. And when one recognizes the angers, guilts and fears generated by stocks, bonds and inheritances, who would say humor cannot help us deal with the emotional involvements related to such money matters?

But what is the underlying tension between eternal investment and worldly greed? Greed never satisfies itself. Desire for money becomes god. The fruit of all that can only be anger, eventually fear and guilt too. The cure? Reducing desire to size by a generous, openhanded spirit. Have you noticed the liberated delight in persons who love to give?

Money studies show that a substantial raise in salary brings adjustment problems, for example, in marriage and family. Sometimes those problems prove severe, even to breaking up a home. While the implications of this research finding are multiple, one factor which stands out is that overextended desire contributes to maladjustment.

Do you remember the children's story about King Midas, who wanted everything he touched to become gold? He got his wish. His eyes lighted with excitement as he touched eggs and watched them turn into money. One object after another glittered and glistened as he put a finger or hand to them. Then he got hungry, but when bread and meat became gold, he couldn't eat yellow metal no matter how precious. The greedy man begged for a return to the life he had once known.

Joy in life resides not in getting so much as in giving. That's why Jesus said it's more blessed to give than to receive. And "blessed" is an old fashioned word for happiness which has a way of coming to those whose angers are redeemed, whose fears are healed, and whose guilts are forgiven.

4 "Primary Reactions" and The Attitude of Joy

St. Paul said we should have no anxiety about anything, but in everything, with prayer and thanksgiving, make our wishes known to God. He goes on to assure us that, with this spirit, God's peace will invade our hearts. Paul loses ability to spell out the depth of this peace; he calls it a calm that "transcends all understanding" (Philippians 4:7, NIV).

Ella Wheeler Wilcox fights fear in this language:

Fate used me meanly; but I looked at her and laughed,

That none might know how bitter was the cup I quaffed.

Along came Joy, and paused beside me where I sat,

Saying, "I came to see what you were laughing at."

The southern humorist, Lewis Grizzard, uses less dignified language. He wrote a book, after his heart surgery, entitled, *They Tore Out My Heart and Stomped That Sucker Flat.*

The science of physiological psychology can measure accelerated or retarded pulse, diminished or increased glandular activity, temperature changes in the body — any of which can stimulate body parts and in turn trigger emotions. So what are the strongest emotions? Most researchers answer: fear, anger and love. These are sometimes called the three "primary reactions." Any of the three can be activated from outward circumstances (external stimuli) or internal thoughts (subjective stimuli). Memory, association or introspection have power to start the flow of fear, anger or love.

John Watson, a pioneer in psychological studies, demonstrated that even infants can experience the three primary emotions.

Another of the pioneer researchers, William James, spoke specifically on what we can do about these emotional reactions: "The greatest discovery of my generation is that human beings can alter their lives by altering their attitudes of mind." We know from experience and intuition, and from scientific laughter studies, that humor is one of nature's instruments for altering attitudes. Thus, the call to action looms clear enough. Engage your psyche with the positives of life, then watch the mind's atmosphere change and in turn one's whole frame of reference.

How Do You Perceive Reality?

Jesus taught us that, "The eye is the lamp of the body. So, if your eye is healthy, your whole body will be full of light; but if your eye is unhealthy," he concludes, "your whole body will be full of darkness." He even says, "If then the light in you is darkness, how great is the darkness!" (Matthew 6:22-23, NRSV).

5

Jesus here talks about the basis of perceived reality. We all see life as essentially friendly or unfriendly, sad or glad, full of disappointment or opportunity. Jesus announces that a happy or unhappy view of life comes from what we see. The practical implication is that we must *choose* to look at the good.

Have you noticed that people who do not believe in happy marriages associate with persons who have a twisted view of family? Likewise, individuals who cannot accept God as a loving heavenly Father identify with those who do not see God as personal. By the same token, all who perceive life as a dirty deal develop a circle of friends who live angry lives.

Psychologists have long known that environment can generate anger or any of the emotions. Fear, anger and resentment cause biochemical changes, and if the negative emotions persist, give rise to behavioral and bodily changes. For example, anger can speed up heart action, send the body into shaking motions, cause temporary blindness or loss of voice. Some grapple with their emotions by putting on a mask of bravado or false humility.

We must say no to escapist ways of handling reality. Change friends and environment — for the people with whom you associate help determine what you see. And what you see shapes your style of perceiving. A joy-filled environment has enormous healing power.

6 Joy Fights Bitterness

Jesus, whose forthright communication has a way of getting through to us, said He intended His words to make us full of joy (John 15:11).

The post-biblical writer, Hermas, caught something of the meaning of Jesus' words when he exhorted, "Put sadness away from thee, for truly sadness is the sister of halfheartedness and bitterness." He says more, "Array thee in the joy that always finds favour in God's sight and is acceptable with him; yea, revel thou therein. For everyone that is joyous worketh and thinketh these things that are good, and despiseth sadness. But he that is sad doth always wickedly; first because he maketh sad the Holy Spirit that hath been given to man for joy; and secondly he worketh lawlessness, in that he neither prays to God nor gives thanks."

Then Hermas comes to his clinching point with a challenge, "Therefore cleanse thyself from this wicked sadness, and thou shalt live with God. Yes, unto God all they shall live who have cast out sadness from themselves, and arrayed themselves in all joy."

What strikes us immediately about this ancient statement is the relation of sadness to wickedness, of the Holy Spirit to cleansing. The power of these second-century words helps us fight bitterness with joy.

Sadness and bitterness can flower from self-sympathy. A woman who lost her husband to a heart attack before retirement developed a chronic bitterness. She nursed the trauma, told God He was unfair, and coddled anger. Result? A personality change. Whereas she had previously lived a loving and outgoing life, never knowing an enemy, now she withdrew into anger. She actually truncated her usefulness and cut off her own peace of mind. Joy has power to reverse that.

The tricky part of trauma like the widow's is that it comes unaware. How then, do we prepare for it? By cultivating in good days joy, laughter and mirth, some of God's chief instruments for faith development.

Faith, like a muscle, builds girth as we school ourselves in positive attitudes. And one of the best ways to strengthen strong spirits is to fight difficulty with deliberate joy. Note that Hermas even says to "revel" in joy.

How to Handle Guilt

Jeremiah 48:33 reveals the judgment of God: "Gladness and joy have been taken away from the fruitful land of Moab; I have stopped the wine from the wine presses; no one treads them with shouts of joy; the shouting is not the shout of joy" (NRSV). Jeremiah depicts God's judgment as the removal of joy.

Moab simply would not face her guilt. Just here lies the reason for the absence of delight in her life.

Our modern world knows two kinds of guilt: real and imagined. Fancied guilt comes either from a too-conscientious spirit or a twisted mind. Laughter can assist in putting our merely supposed guilts to rest. But real guilt, as Moab experienced, needs forthright confession and the accompanying willingness to make amends.

Laughter, of course, will not solve wrongdoing. One of the subtle tragedies of our time is what we may call "covering laughter," which attempts to persuade people to believe that wrong is right and right is wrong. Modern drama, telecommunications and cinema will have much to answer for at Judgment Day!

The clear message of the Scriptures from beginning to end is simply that the guiltless have joy, and the guilty suffer dejection. Sad or glad? That's a basic biblical question. And unique to biblical theology is the heartening promise that the guilty need not stay that way. When God forgives our guilt, He forgets it and we can too.

One more piece of the picture is that Moab refused to admit her guilt. Pretense yields rotten fruit — maladjustment. The tricky factor is that Moab thought she could get away with sin (Jeremiah 48). She found out differently.

Willingness to see the whole picture is the launching pad for confession, which in turn gives birth to fresh beauty and gladness.

IX

Communication with Joy

*"Humor is essentially **social**.
When we hear a joke, we immediately want
to tell it to others.
When we enjoy a joke in an audience situation, we tend to turn
to our fellows and share our
enjoyment with them."*
— Robert T. Oliver,
The Psychology of Persuasive Speech

*"Laughter is the shortest
distance between two people."*
— Victor Borge

Have a Good Laugh

King Duncan and Angela Akres tell about the little boy in Sunday school class who heard the story of the wedding at Cana and how Jesus turned water into wine.

Once home, the little fellow's dad asked him what he learned from the wedding story. He thought awhile, then answered: "If you're having a wedding, make sure Jesus is there."

1 You Yourself

Psalm 57 is the cry of a man hurting deeply, "I cry to God Most High. ... He will send from heaven and save me. ... God will send forth his steadfast love and his faithfulness!" (verses 2-3, NRSV). The clear note of joy and faith rings right through David's misery. He's realistic but not self-sympathizing.

Helen Hayes and her husband, Charles MacArthur, lost their 19-year-old daughter to polio. Charlie died a few years later, but Helen lived productively into her 80s. Her own explanation reveals that Charlie never quit asking, "Why should it happen to us? We didn't do anything to anybody. We never hurt anybody. Why? Why? Why?" Helen, seeing other people in tragedy, asked, "Why not us?"

The complexities of human nature and thought outstrip our abilities to analyze, much less judge. So whether or not the great actress spoke accurately we cannot know, but surely she was right in insisting on a positive attitude.

One's basic attitude comes through in communication. Some can mask their real attitudes but not for long. Most of our communication comes through body language, what the professionals call kinesics and another part is tone. The least impactful element is language. Since body language and tone do not submit to rehearsal as easily as words, they are unconscious instruments of self-disclosure and they subtly reveal our identity. What we *are* communicates first, last and loudest.

Helen Hayes' basic joy comes through even as she relates her tragedy. Her very manner tells us much about her positive posture.

The ethical character of a communicator carries enormous weight. The Incarnation is an eloquent example, and that explains S.D. Gordon's statement that, "Jesus is God spelling himself out in language that man can understand." The bottom line is that we trust Jesus because we know His integrity.

When Phillips Brooks defined preaching as truth through personality, he articulated the incarnational principle of communication. When the psalmist says right out that he's hurting, God respects that honesty. When Helen Hayes reveals her faith, she exposes her heart and therefore communicates her very self.

S.D. Gordon, author of more than 20 devotional books, sums up in one simple sentence the principle that you yourself communicate: "The way from God to a human heart is through a human heart." Joy-filled hearts communicate with peculiar power.

Enthusiasm

2

Proverbs 15:23 puts rich meaning and truth in this language, "To make an apt answer is a joy to anyone, and a word in season, how good it is!" (NRSV). When we say the right thing at the right time, delight and enthusiasm characterize our communication.

Norman Vincent Peale asked, why do we remember some writers, speakers and leaders forever? "For their ability, leadership qualities and achievements, of course," he began; then added, "but one important reason is their boundless enthusiasm and the joy they took in life and in the world."

Enthusiasm literally means to be inspired or possessed by God. When we talk about inspired speech we refer to enriched and heightened stimulus. The ancients saw that as godly. God puts Himself in our communication when we rouse others to think noble thoughts and stir people to good deeds.

Listen to what three Samuels say about enthusiasm. Samuel Chadwick, the English Methodist preacher, says that, "Men ablaze are invincible. The stronghold of Satan is proof against everything but fire."

Samuel Goldwyn, movie producer says that, "Enthusiasm is the key not only to the achievement of great things but to the accomplishment of anything that is worthwhile."

Finally, Sam Jones, the American evangelist, says that, "A horse that will pull on a cold collar will do to depend on — and the best Christians are those who never need 'warming up'."

Those three snippets represent a whole literature of enthusiasm in the Western World. Animated address has a contagion about it. In fact, we can make very ordinary comments in a framework of delighted animation, and they will carry genuine thrusts of meaning.

Enthusiasm and joy are Siamese twins. One cannot move without the other. The two can be quiet or outgoing in manner, but they will create momentum. When the Spirit of God is the Author of that enthusiasm and joy, they set hearts afire and in the flame mere words translate into reality. That is communication.

Robert Murray McCheyne cries, "O Lord, evermore give us this enthusiasm!"

Another son of Scotland, James S. Stewart, spoke with equal fervor, "The supreme need of the church is the same in the twentieth century as in the first; it is men on fire for Christ."

Have you noticed that wherever you encounter that mood of enthusiasm, the joy of the Lord comes alive?

Communication Overload

The classic passage on God's communication with Elijah finds summary in these cogent words, "And behold, the Lord passed by, and a great and strong wind rent the mountains, and broke in pieces the rocks before the Lord, but the Lord was not in the wind; and after the wind an earthquake, but the Lord was not in the earthquake; and after the earthquake a fire, but the Lord was not in the fire." Then comes the unexpected, "and after the fire a still small voice" (1 Kings 19:11b-12, RSV). Everyone knows the quiet voice came from God.

The *Superwoman* news sheet came to life in retaliation against "rock-breaking winds," those fire-and-earth communiqués, all saying today's woman can be super everything. She can smell like a flower garden 24 hours a day, rear children without emotional hang-ups, keep her husband happy, work 50 hours a week or more, and maintain her equilibrium through it all. *Superwoman* says "no" to all that. It says women must find quiet spaces in their lives if they expect to keep their balance. It's OK to go around without a burden of guilt that there's something undone.

Both men and women, and now children, have succumbed to our 20th century communication overload, no doubt in reaction to an earlier era when so many embraced a lazy and chaotic lifestyle. Today our problem is not only different but doubled in intensity. The very vehicles of communication announcing we can be superpersons clamor for attention with rock-breaking, earthquake sounds and flashing signals of fire. A kind of rock-and-roll bombast characterizes the TV commercials, the garish highway signboards, the loud and fast radio ads, and the demands of information age computers.

But God's communications often come quietly. We sense them in the touch of a little child's hand, the awesome stillness of a wooded hiking trail, a silent sunrise, a book by a winter's fire, or the inner voice. What strikes the listener attuned to God's voice is the comfort, strength and joy that always accompany it.

4 Humor in Speeches

The book of Proverbs has a great deal to say about speech. Whether we hear advice for private or public speech, the passages sum up this way: the speaker must come across as both appropriate and wise.

Note "appropriate and wise" ways to employ humor. When a good laugh puts your audience at ease, you have constructed a bridge between yourself and your people. The bridge puts both audience and speaker at ease.

The best wit flows out of one's ordinary conversation. That's what works best in public settings. If, for example, you tell jokes well, you're probably a sure ringer for telling them to a group. But woe to the leader who can't tell funny stories but tries anyway.

Both Steve Allen and Art Linkletter warn against off-color jokes. After all, God and good sense call us to exercise judgment in sharing stories and not just about dirty stories. One must use critical faculties when sizing up the background and setting of the audience (church, school, club, whatever), the occasion (humor at a funeral? Sometimes), and the group mood (you can hitchhike on a contagious, mirth-filled atmosphere). "Fitness" is crucial: when the feel of a story or humor line fits like your hand in a glove, you've got a winner.

Playful kidding ("roasting"), often "in" today, must come to life with reserve, and depends on your own gifts as a public person and the dignity of the person you're ribbing. You don't kid the university dean unless he, you and the circumstances permit it.

Authenticity is the key to successful public humor. If your joke or real-life story has the ring of truth about it, if it meshes with reality, people identify and respond appropriately. If, on the other hand, artifice comes through, if the audience gets the idea you have calculated your measured phrases just to get a laugh, the reaction will reflect displeasure.

Above all, let your humor suggest the joy Christians know. The essence of the early Christian witness was radiance. Of a godly person, someone commented, "His smiles were fraught with greater meaning than his sermons."

Communication for Learning

The Bible exhorts us to learn. Knowledge, when married to wisdom, yields the rewards of joy and fulfillment. The Bible writers would express pleasure at the advances in 20th century education, not only in terms of information but inspiration as well.

However, Scripture writers would resonate with the "dangerous nonsense" thesis of Neil Postman's *Amusing Ourselves to Death: Public Disclosure in the Age of Show Business*. After all, we do need to think clearly. Television, the New York University professor of communications believes, has made our American talk "shriveled and absurd" and tends to reduce our culture to mere entertainment.

What the Bible would not agree with is the oft-heard statement in our time that culture and learning cannot advance in an era of pictures. The Bible itself is a pictographic book. Modern brain research documents that the vast majority of people do picture-thinking, the way most everyone learns.

Actually, education has done a turnabout. Educators once came at their task only with great seriousness; now we know that learning can come wrapped in amusing packages. Researchers discovered teachers from the elementary level to graduate school using humor, film, games — all sorts of fun vehicles — as means of measurable learning. Educational TV is the most obvious example of the learning-can-be-fun movement, and now our classrooms and churches use camera, screen and projector.

Research demonstrates that school children may listen and learn better in the presence of humor. Fast-paced humor proved, in some research, a better vehicle for capturing adolescents' attention. TV, books and magazines can all use humor to educational advantage. But the use of humor enhances video learning, where the stimulus to laugh works with musical background and entertainment props as support mechanisms. Situations and circumstances differ, of course, and much research must still come to completion. But Dolf Zillmann and Jennings Bryant, in "Uses and Effects of Humor in Educational Ventures," a chapter in Volume II of the *Handbook of Humor Research*, indicate not only the complexities of humor usage in learning, but also that well-used mirth can function as a facilitator of genuine education.

A Way of Communicating Help

St. Paul, in his prison epistle, Philippians, uses words like *joy, thanks, rejoice.* As it turns out, that little book is ministry, especially to people in a bind of some sort.

Humor can fill people with joy and thus be genuine ministry. Every human being feels at some time or another the aggression people use to get their own way. The heaviness of that feeling can be diffused by a story or a single line that elicits laughter. For example, little children get pretty demanding. One might tell the W.C. Fields pun. "Mr. Fields," someone asked, "do you believe in clubs for children?"

"Only when kindness fails," he replied.

Again, humor is a marvelous balm when life's contradictions shackle us. To reduce the heaviness of incongruities to size is a great service. "It's not the passages in Scripture I cannot understand that bother me," said Mark Twain. "It's the passages I do understand that trouble me." Mark Twain had a way of making fog go away, while at the same time facing up to life's conundrums.

Think about humor as release from the mounting tensions of life. One suspects that, at base, we created parties for gaiety to help us handle stress. Sometimes that gaiety advances best simply by sharing funny experiences.

What we share often comes right out of our daily experience. Like the couple who invited a new friend for dinner. Knowing his usual promptness, they worried when he did not show up. Finally he rang the doorbell and reported on his difficult time finding the house. "I drove up and down your street," he said, "looking for 1492. But your address is 1776."

Laughter as Communication

7

Laughter studies, as we think of them today, originated only recently. Psychologists began their inquiries in 1928, and theologians have also done some research and writing in the last few years. Philologists probably entered the arena most recently. But one factor they all seem to agree on is that, laughter, at root, is a method of communication.

And a powerful medium, too. Jesus' comment about the log and the speck (Matthew 7:5), a species of humor called irony, tells us about judging. It says that guilty people love to divert attention away from their own sins by pointing out the mistakes of others.

Dickens' ingenious description of London's fog-and-smoke covering, exposes not the evils of coal burning (the clean-air movement would come later), but what George F. Will of the *Washington Post* calls the "choking legal system" of the day. People who see behind the figure cannot help but smile.

Or take Oscar Wilde's scathing play, *The Importance of Being Earnest*, his masterpiece of 1895. Wilde uncovers the hypocrisy and raw inconsistencies of society for all to see, much to the delight of theatergoers. He intends to expose appearance for appearance's sake, to ridicule people who take trivial matters seriously, and to put sincerity and earnestness into perspective. The play strikes one as very funny, just the impression the writer intended.

Jesus, Dickens and Wilde tell us that when people cannot hear by direct communication, indirect talk, especially when coated with the frosting of humor, can make truth palatable. Let's face it: when something tastes good it goes down easier.

**"This is Sherry's answering service.
Please leave your name, age, length of hair and
whether or not you have an earring at the sound of the beep."**

The Joy of Creativity

*"Claudel, the French poet,
said after listening to
Beethoven's Fifth Symphony
that he knew now that
at the heart of the universe
there was joy."*

— Gerald Kennedy

Have a Good Laugh

A plumber wrote a government agency about the use of hydrochloric acid to clean sewer pipes. "Can it do harm?"

The plumber got this reply: "The efficacy of hydrochloric acid is indisputable, but the corrosive residue is incompatible with metallic permanence."

The plumber thanked the research bureau for saying OK to his technique.

The distraught authorities wrote once more: "We cannot assume responsibility for the production of toxic and noxious residue with hydrochloric acid and suggest you use an alternative procedure."

Once again the delighted plumber thanked the government department for approval. Now the authorities squirmed nervously and ordered still another memo sent to the plumber.

The last memorandum read: "Do not use hydrochloric acid. It eats living daylights out of the pipes."

1 The Freedom to Create

St. Paul writes, "Now the Lord is the Spirit, and where the Spirit of the Lord is, there is freedom" (2 Corinthians 3:17, NRSV). Paul might have ended the verse this way — *there is freedom and creativity* — for where the Spirit of the Lord is both appear.

Plautus, a Roman playwright who lived before Christ, paints a clown in his drama, *Pseudolus*. The buffoon (Pseudolus) has red hair, a potbelly, legs like a piano, a big head, pointed eyes, darkish skin, very large feet and a red face. Although Pseudolus is a slave, in the play he enjoys absolute freedom. Superior to his master, he is the writer, analogous to the real writer, Plautus. In the monologue of act one he puts pen to paper and creates a plot. "I'll play the playwright," he shouts in the spirit of freedom and fun.

That freedom to imagine is the seed of great joy. Actually, to imagine constructively results in multiplied joy and is the base of much humor. An important difference between Christian and secular humor, however, relates to freedom's boundaries. The Christian cannot use freedom to unleash human impulses at will, for twisted drives find their rootage in evil. Making light in implied approval of drink, promiscuity, violence or other evil results ultimately not in creativity but discreativity. To laugh at God's laws is final imprisonment.

On the other hand, to poke innocent fun at our

weaknesses to employ surprise, incongruity and exag-
geration, to allow sanctified imagination to roam for joy
and build for character development — this is authentic
liberty and brings not a sour but a happy taste to one's
spirit.

To assume the freedom offered in Christ to innovate
in the daily round, the workplace, the recreation setting —
this sets the stage for optimum fulfillment.

Music from a Cheerful Heart

2

The frequently quoted Proverbs 15:13 fits Franz
Joseph Haydn perfectly: "A glad heart makes a cheerful
countenance, but by sorrow of heart the spirit is broken"
(NRSV). Haydn declared, "God gave me a cheerful heart,
so He will surely forgive me if I serve Him cheerfully."

"The music of Haydn," says one music critic, "has
cheer, beauty, logic, order, nobility, freshness of imagination and humor." Little wonder he appears on concert
programs with frequency.

What accounts for such fundamental joy in the great
composer's scores? The answer, simple yet profound,
goes right to the heart of God and creation. He perceived
God as sovereign; he saw nature not as chaotic but ordered. Thus the superficial and transient glamour, tragedy and excitements of the world carried little weight
with Franz.

But Haydn got his foundational philosophy from
the Bible. That Book he believed, must form the basis of all
he did including politics, religion, education, his entire
lifestyle. To accept the Scriptural rationale for all of life
meant to find freedom; to deny that basis resulted in imprisonment.

The great composer did not use that theological
basis as an escape device, as some have tried to do in the
crises of life. Rather, he faced difficulties. In them God gave
him cheer, and from the commingling of tragedy and joy
his music flowed in a never-ending stream of creativity.

As a boy studying music, he did all sorts of pranks and had fun. On one occasion he simply could not say no to the temptation to cut off the pigtail of a singer in the choir. The choirmaster ousted him, but he never lost his child's heart for mirth. His music documents his humor.

But much militated against the maintenance of that merriment. Composition always came hard for him, but his disciplined regularity overcame what could easily have developed into laziness. Not only could his wife bear no children, but sadly, she had absolutely no appreciation for her husband's work. Unbelievably, she used his manuscripts for pastry papers and hair curlers.

Out of all this came an original, the giant who created the symphony and string quartet as we know them today. Mozart gave him the right nickname, "Papa Haydn."

Franz Joseph did not aim to make a big new splash in the musical world. He simply wanted to make people happy. He wished to help people substitute a smile for a frown and to see their disappointments through fresh eyes.

He sensed God's hands upon his own as he composed. Daily, as he put together the *Creation*, "I fell on my knees and asked God for strength." In 1808, then an old man, Haydn heard a public performance of the *Creation*. When the mighty chorus rendered, "And There was Light," Haydn's hands lifted heavenward and he whispered, "Not from me. It all comes from above."

And just there lies the Source of all good, including a cheerful and creative heart.

The Joy of Creative Answers

She was technically a good tennis player, but something evaded her. The instructor, a creative spirit, studied her game and then came up with a suggestion that proved innovative and timely. He asked, "Do you know the 'Blue Danube Waltz'?" She did. "Then, as we play, I want you to time your strokes to the rhythm of 'The Blue Danube Waltz'."

She hummed the tune as she volleyed. Her forehand and backhand began to find their tempo. Then her movements flowed. Flowed, I suspect, rather like a ballet dancer.

When she stopped, joy wrote itself on her face, says Norman Vincent Peale in telling the remarkable results. She exclaimed, "I never felt the joy and thrill of this game before. For the first time in my life I feel I can master it." A creative idea had helped her find her own rhythm and harmony and therefore an improved game.

The Living Bible renders Galatians 5:22-23 like this, "But when the Holy Spirit controls our lives he will produce this kind of fruit in us: love, joy, peace, patience, kindness, goodness, faithfulness, gentleness and self-control. ..." The Spirit's control is the basis of creativity and the origin of sound problem solving. And the inward result? Satisfaction, the joy Paul describes.

I have a friend with high blood pressure, the result of his very busy executive life. When he feels pulled in more directions than he can handle, he sometimes goes fishing. Driving 30 miles into the nearby mountains, he stops his car at a favorite spot, pulls on his wading boots, takes rod and reel into the river, and forgets his problems. The gentle lapping of the water against the shore, the never-ending flow of the river, the songs of the birds, and the wind in the trees — the whole mix of outdoor experiences restores him.

One day, after fishing in the mountains, he went to the doctor. The physician stated in astonishment, "Your blood pressure is nearly normal." This creative solution, born of God's creativity, had restored my friend.

As he told me about this, the joy in his voice and the delightful look on his face led me to believe he would go fishing again and again.

The Joy of Creative Closure

The close of Book IV of the Psalms reads like this, "Blessed be the Lord, the God of Israel, from everlasting to everlasting. And let all the people say, 'Amen!' Praise the Lord!" (Psalms 106:48, NRSV). Actually, quite a number of the psalms end in similar fashion, not always in doxology, but often with that special sense of closure reflecting joyous fulfillment.

What we must notice is that as frequently as a psalm terminates in closure, the body of the chapter has struggled with an issue — usually a warring crisis in battle or in the soul. The reader can watch the dialogue of the psalmist, then see him come to a creative conclusion by the power of God's Spirit.

That pattern of dialogue prior to the final resolution models the mind's workings. Blaise Pascal observed the Yes-No-Final Answer movement of the mind in problem-solving. He informed us that this is the way God made us to handle challenges. Interior conversation is one way we create, for all creativity is really problem solving.

The problem is that the dialogue can stimulate us so much we rob ourselves of the sheer joy of coming to decisions. Take the matter of a new job. What delight we really experience in a fresh environment, different colleagues and perspectives on work not thought of before! The whole change of coloration holds potential for gladdening the heart. Yet we miss that if we ask questions *ad infinitim* and never really decide for the new employment.

Neurosis is indecision. Therapists know the negative impact of uncertainty. This is not to say we should engage in careless decision making. To the contrary, the more we involve ourselves in the hard business of clear thinking, the greater the joy when at last we come down on the point of closure.

The Art of the Child

Jesus, sharing with His disciples who had asked about greatness, said, "Truly I say to you, unless you change and become like children, you will never enter the kingdom of heaven. Whoever becomes humble like this child is the greatest in the kingdom of heaven" (Matthew 18:3, NRSV).

In the whole of his 35 years, Wolfgang Amadeus Mozart never lost the little child in him. His playful mind created constantly. He could not think of mundane matters like running a household. Instead, he filled his head with rhythms, notations, harmonies, sequences and motifs. With the excitement of a little child getting ready to go on a journey, he put his creations on score paper.

Musicologists agree that Mozart had more music in him than any composer. God made him to create. Songs, traceries and variations fairly leaped from his brain onto paper. The graceful dancelike character of his compositions made him the most popular composer of all time. "Composing," he confessed, "is my one joy and passion."

Mozart had fun with his public. He loved watching reactions to his music. The gliding grace of his sounds, tones and rhythms slid right into the hearts of his listeners, lifted them to new heights and left them saying, "Life's a happy affair after all."

Today doctors would probably diagnose Wolfgang Amadeus as hyperactive. He simply could not sit still or keep quiet. He sang, jumped about, rollicked with laughter, even when others could see no humor. His genius absorbed everything musical — compositional forms, national norms, cultural overtones — and this mix translated into grand sounds. He wrote over 600 pieces of music.

Father of the modern concerto, he also performed the first piano concerto publicly. But whether he played or wrote he came across as a singer. Song was the center of his creativity, especially in his later years. He loved to write in the garden, listening to the songbirds. He used varied colors of ink on his scores. The transparency of his music is like a clear running brook.

Mozart loved life. He wrote *The Marriage of Figaro* which established the comic opera for time to come. Opera lent itself to the humor and excitement he saw in life. "I never lie down at night," said this genius, "without reflecting that, young as I am, I may not live to see another day. Yet no one of all my acquaintances could say that in company I am morose or disgruntled. For this blessing I daily thank my Creator."

The source and center of his faith was that Creator. Sometimes writers portray him without much faith, but Mozart aimed to reflect God. And the joy of the Almighty's creation shines through unclouded. Like a little child, Mozart never got over the wonder of God's world.

We cannot write music like Mozart, but we can cultivate his sense of wonder, source of joyous creativity, in whatever we do.

Creativity and Disappointments

In a great, grand passage on the redemption of Israel, Jeremiah burst into song: "Then shall the young women rejoice in the dance, and the young men and the old shall be merry. I will turn their mourning into joy, I will comfort them, and give them gladness for sorrow" (Jeremiah 31:13, NRSV).

Ludwig von Beethoven, keenly aware of God's sovereignty in the midst of sorrow, saw the Almighty as his Comfort, Authority and Source of talent. He prayed on one occasion that he felt "called upon to produce" music. "Divine One," he cried, "thou lookest into my inmost soul, thou knowest it, thou knowest that love of man and desire to good live therein."

Yet Beethoven lived a tragic life. Deafness turned him inward. A nephew he tried to rear with tenderness and love turned out poorly. Ludwig was a loner by nature. But nothing kept him from composing marvelously exuberant music.

Frank Gaebelein, in his excellent essay, "Beethoven: A Bicentennial Tribute," observed that, because Beethoven "translated his Job-like experience into tone, musical literature has no more profound statement of the problem of suffering and its resolution than his."

Then Gaebelein relates the powerful story of Geoffery Bull, English missionary tortured by the Chinese Communists. Bull says that even though his captors robbed him of his Bible and made him face the possibility of death, that when Beethoven's *Emperor Concerto* came wafting into his cell from a nearby radio, it brought such refreshment the prisoner could confront anything. The gripping story comes from Mr. Bull's well-known, *When Iron Gates Yield.*

Ludwig could write *scherzos* (jokes). He could put witticisms into music; his rondos are famous for that. He expressed struggle, of course. Similar to the book of Psalms, he ranged over the human stretches of life and emotion, and that helps explain the universal love of his works.

One concert pianist summarizes Beethoven's music and the joy it brings with incisive accuracy: "... as you listen ... thank God for this man whose music speaks so eloquently of struggle with affliction, of the joy and humor of life, of sorrow and consolation, and serenity that surmounts suffering."

Art, like humor, sometimes grows out of adversity. People who use their disappointments as instruments of creativity bring joy not only to themselves but to many others.

One mother in constant pain helped start a Christian day school, and she herself taught in it. No one could associate with her and miss her genuine happiness.

God's Creativity

Ezekiel 37, the classic passage on the dry bones, describes those bones as "very dry."

"Can these bones live?" is the crucial question. The answer, "Thus says the Lord God to these bones: I will cause breath to enter you, and you shall live" (Ezekiel 37:5, NRSV).

Have you noticed God's creative genius in bringing life out of death, order out of chaos, and good out of evil? Mother Teresa, a Nobel Peace Prize-winner, says God uses us to bring about His creative products.

How? By *"loving as He loves,*
helping as He helps,
giving as He gives,
serving as He serves,
rescuing as He rescues,
being with Him for all the twenty-four hours,
touching Him in His distressing disguise."
That "distressing disguise" is the clincher. When Mother Teresa confronts a particularly stubborn person, she says only that he or she is Jesus in a "distressing disguise."

Joy, says Mother Teresa, is the characteristic by which God uses us to remake the distressing into the desired, the discreative into the creative. "Joy is prayer — Joy is strength — Joy is love — Joy is a net of love by which you can catch souls." The person "gives most who gives with joy."

So God takes bad situations and makes them good, and He uses us to help Him. He uses us best when we accept our assignments with joy. Test that law for yourself. When you discover its solid truth, your faith will elevate. That strengthened belief in God's creative faithfulness will gladden your heart and in turn make you God's joyful helper.

XI

Nature and Beauty

"A thing of beauty is a joy forever."
— John Keats

"Never lose an opportunity
of seeing anything that is
beautiful; for beauty is God's
handwriting — a wayside sacrament.
Welcome it in every fair face,
in every fair sky,
in every fair flower,
and thank God for it
as a cup of blessing."
— Ralph Waldo Emerson

Have a Good Laugh

This time, with George Burns:

❖ He wants someone to invent a chemically treated mailbox that will self-destruct!

❖ He also wants doctors to pay for parking fees patients must pay for waiting a couple hours!

❖ A sign of old age: When you like crowds because they keep you from falling down.

1 Informality Within Structure

In Search of Excellence reveals that one mark of successful corporations is informality; another mark is structure. Over and again in the book, these twin motifs raise their hands for recognition. Productive management has learned something from nature. We do indeed find structure in nature, but not rigidly so. For example, trees are structurally similar; however, can you imagine all trees looking alike, all terribly neat with no straggly branches, only straight wood and leaves with strict look-alike coloration?

Have you watched ducks dive into a lake? They use the wind currents as slides and, upon hitting the water, see how far they can coast. They relish fun. Such fun, mirth and humor mark much of nature. And nature is a role model for human beings.

Out of informality, fun and spontaneity a higher framework of order arises. If the duck spent all her time keeping the ducklings clean and neat, she could not be the unencumbered creature she is. People who overextend the principle of order render themselves disordered and thus quell the very creativity for which God made them.

Throughout *In Search of Excellence*, authors Peters and Waterman state that the highest creativity and best productivity come out of a free and open workplace where management, atmosphere and even furnishings suggest that *anything* is possible. Companies confined to straight-line procedures have a lower achievement record.

The principle of informality within structure spells excitement. And excitement creates fun, joy and pride in accomplishment.

True Happiness, True Grief

St. Paul tells us victory swallows death and quotes the famous Hosea passage: "Where, O death, is your victory? Where, O grave, your sting?" Then he adds, "The sting of death is sin, and the power of sin is the law. But thanks be to God, who gives us the victory through our Lord Jesus Christ" (1 Corinthians 15:54-57, NRSV). This statement typifies the death passages of the New Testament, and we stand amazed that joy is their hallmark. Yes, death is an enemy, and it is the occasion for grief, but the divinity in death strikes us with such impact, with so much authenticity, that Christians find themselves rejoicing.

Paul Tournier, referring to his late wife, Nelly, said, "I can truly say that I have a great grief and that I am a happy man." He confessed that he missed their times of meditation most, and that prior to her death he sometimes forgot his private devotional period, but since her homegoing had not missed a single day. In those times of spiritual focus, Dr. Tournier felt the nearness of his wife.

This sense of closeness is common. Norman Vincent Peale wrote about it in *Plus* magazine, in the article, "When Loved Ones Leave Us." He also spelled this out in his *Treasury of Joy and Enthusiasm*, and in his autobiography, *The True Joy of Positive Living*, he even refers to a laughter experience at a funeral!

One of the most interesting phenomena Christians face is laughter in the presence of death. More than release of tension, it reveals what God built into us — the fact of heaven, a place where no tears or evil can exist. Peter Berger believes the comic is heaven breaking through. When my friend Ralph Turnbull died, I realized contentment, deep joy, from the moment the word came to me by phone. The reason is clear enough: Ralph now lives in heaven.

Freud hit upon something more profound than he may have known when he said, "We can lose nothing without replacing it." That is a law of nature. Nothing can really come to destruction; it may take another shape, but ultimately it resurrects in new life. For example, the land around Mount St. Helens sprouted a rich vegetation shortly after volcanic eruptions.

The knowledge of resurrection, new life and heaven is a strong basis for holy hilarity.

3 Nature's Joy

The Living Bible renders the last paragraph of Psalm 65 (verses 6-13) with immense joy. In verse 8: "The dawn and sunset shout for joy!" Verses 11-12: "Then he crowns it all with green, lush pastures in the wilderness; hillsides blossom with joy." The paragraph's close: "All the world shouts with joy, and sings."

Charles Spurgeon picked up on Scripture's joy in nature when he wrote, "Doth not all nature around me praise God? If I were silent, I should be an exception to the universe."

John Burroughs, the naturalist, says that if he had to name the three chief resources of life, they would be books, friends and nature. He adds that "at least the most constant and always at hand, is nature."

Nature "moves the heart, appeals to the mind, and fires the imagination — health to the body, a stimulus to the intellect, and joy to the soul." Burroughs explains: "To the scientist, nature is a storehouse of facts, laws, processes; to the artist she is a storehouse of pictures; to the poet she is a storehouse of images, fancies, a source of inspiration; to the moralist she is a storehouse of precepts and parables; to all she may be a source of knowledge and joy."

Though blind since infancy, Helen Keller penned a poem entitled, "In the Garden of the Lord," in which she shapes this remarkable line: "I laugh and shout for life is good."

The same spirit controlled Elizabeth Barrett Browning's pen when she wrote,

> *Earth's crammed with heaven,*
> *And every common bush afire with God.*

The 18th century evangelicals saw nature as God's signature. Autographs say something about personality, and God's signature tells us He loves us. Otherwise, why give us all this beauty? To see love and beauty in nature is to know true joy. In turn we want to praise the Creator.

God Cares for the Birds

Jesus said, "Look at the birds of the air: they neither sow nor reap nor gather into barns, and yet your heavenly Father feeds them" (Matthew 6:26, NRSV). God seems to take special delight in taking care of His own. The birds, yes — and us too.

We have a birdfeeder in our backyard near the kitchen windows, from which we can observe our feathered friends. We sometimes laugh at the bluejays; their size and cocky manner make smaller birds fly away — except for cardinals. They wear brilliant colors, and they have their rights!

After bluejays and cardinals have their feed, the sparrows and finches return. In the end, all get enough to eat.

"Nature is man's religious book," declared Theodore Parker, "with lessons for every day." One lesson we cannot overlook is that God takes care of us.

And notice another lesson: birds don't give up easily. They come again and again to the feeder, no matter how formidable the opposition. "All problems become smaller if you don't dodge them but confront them," according to William Halsey. He goes on: "Touch a thistle timidly, and it pricks you; grasp it boldly, and its spines crumble."

Freedom and laughter, a certain bold delight in life, accompany the courage to beard the lion in his den. Timidity, paralysis and lack of humor go together and rob one of victory-over-the-thistle. Can you imagine a bird, discouraged and laying down on the job? We can only see birds energetically taking God at His word. We all observe and hear their joy in life.

> By shallow rivers, to whose falls,
> Melodious birds sing madrigals.

— Christopher Marlow
(1564-1593)

5 Stars

Job heard God use these words: "... when the morning stars sang together and all heavenly beings shouted for joy" (Job 38:7, NRSV). Nature brings its own joy and therapy.

W.H. Auden told us that parents have a duty to teach their children the lessons of nature. Nature's creatures have their own identity and can never lose them, he observed, "because they can only be what they already are: the flowers 'fresh and laughing as on the days of great battles,' the beasts who 'walk the earth, ignorant, while their splendor lasts, of any weakness,' and, most of all," concludes the great writer, "the stars of the night sky, in all their unchanging majesty and stateliness of movement."

Astronomer Johannes Kepler, viewing the heavens, saw star clusters at night and cried, "O God, I think thy thoughts after thee." The magnificence of the night sky recaptures our perspective about God, restores our relationship with Him, and puts joy in our hearts. Why would it not? After all, a Being who could create and manage such a universe can only put fresh strength and renewed motivation into us.

William Beebe, a naturalist, used to visit Theodore
Roosevelt. On evenings, after good conversation at
Sagamore Hill, Roosevelt's home, the two walked on the
lawn, looked up at the stars, and then one or the other
would go through their customary ritual:

"That is the Spiral Galaxy of Andromeda. It is as
large as our Milky Way. It is one of a hundred million
galaxies.
It is 750,000 light-years away. It consists of one hundred
billion suns, each larger than our sun."

Then followed silence. Finally Mr. Roosevelt would
say, "Now I think we are small enough. Let's go to bed."

The great God has His ways of showing strength, of
communicating goodness, truth and beauty. The moral
ought within and the starry heavens above speak with
peculiar eloquence. The reminder of this brings deep
settled peace which is also joy.

Give

Jesus told us to "give and it will be given to you; a
good measure, pressed down, shaken together, running
over, will be put into your lap; for the measure you give
will be the measure you get back" (Luke 6:38, NRSV). This
law of life we see illustrated in nature. She always gives
and forever receives.

Jesus also asked us to lend, expecting nothing in
return. Nature never calculates the cost of her giving; she
just gives — and returns come spontaneously. "Blessed
are those who can give without remembering," declared a
large hearted soul, "and take without forgetting."

Elton Trueblood came to the heart of joy's dynamic
when he announced, "A man has made at least a start on
discovering the meaning of human life when he plants
shade trees under which he knows full well he will never
sit."

Calculated giving ends in sorrow and sadness,
cynicism and criticism; but uncomputed giving, by its

very nature, yields gladness.

The ancient Maimonides created "The Golden Ladder of Giving," which shows our potential growth toward liberated, joyful giving:

(1) To give reluctantly, the gift of the hand, but not the heart.

(2) To give cheerfully, but not in proportion to need.

(3) To give cheerfully and proportionately, but not until solicited.

(4) To give cheerfully, proportionately and unsolicited, but to put the gift into the poor man's hand, thus creating shame.

(5) To give in such a way that the distressed may know their benefactor, without being known to them.

(6) To know the objects of our bounty, but remain unknown to them.

(7) To give so that the benefactor may not know those relieved, and they not know him.

(8) To prevent poverty by teaching a trade, setting a man up in business, or in some other way preventing the need of charity.

Dear Lord, rob me of all selfishness, and in its place put the generosity that expects nothing but accepts with gratitude and joy everything You send. *Amen.*

7 Truth, Beauty and Freedom

When Jesus announced that He was the way, the truth and the life, He made clear for all time the chief source of happiness. For to find the truth is to find freedom. And to discover truth is to open one's eyes to beauty:

'Beauty is truth, truth beauty,' — that is all
Ye know on earth, and all ye need to know.
—John Keats

Legalism will not open one to truth and beauty. How right John Baillie, the Scottish theologian, when he said, "The New Testament does not say, 'You shall know the rules, and by them you shall be bound,' but, 'You shall know the truth, and the truth shall make you free.'" Joy degenerates in prison; happiness multiplies in freedom. And only truth can make us free.

"Knowledge is happiness," said Helen Keller, "because to have knowledge — broad deep knowledge — is to know true ends from false, and lofty things from low." Learn the benchmarks of human progress, she counsels. Then you will "feel the great heartthrobs" of the centuries. And if one does sense these pulsations? One hears heaven's harmonies and sees earth's potentialities.

Learn truth. It will open your eyes and liberate them to see beauty everywhere. Take, for example, the truth about humor. Astonishing is its omission in most books on management, in nearly all volumes on health, in virtually every tome on theology. But those who learn the simple truth that things go better with laughter, have opened themselves to a quality and beauty in relationships that facilitate commerce and health, and enhance all living.

Of course, the prior, the basic, truth is Jesus Christ Himself. And how wondrous the freedom that goes with the beauty in Christ!

Samuel Rutherford made joyous freedom known as vividly as anyone could: "Jesus Christ came into my prison cell last night, and every stone flashed like a ruby." There you have the practical benefit of the wisdom that has power to emancipate any circumstance and adorn any setting.

"I see you've taught Junior High before."

XII

Children, Youth and Family

*"A happy family is but
an earlier heaven."*

— John Bowring

Have a Good Laugh

A man from England came to America and made many friends.

On the eve of his return to the British Isles, his friends gave him a good-bye party at a fancy hotel. The emcee stunned the crowd by announcing that he must make a confession: "For over 20 years I was in the arms of another man's wife." After a long pause, he said, to the delight and relief of everyone, "That was my mother."

The Englishman laughed late but heartily, and said to himself, "I must tell that story sometime."

Back in England, his friends threw a welcome-home party. In the middle of the banquet, he remembered the joke and stood to his feet to make his "confession."

"For over 20 years I was in the arms of another man's wife." The pause settled in after oh's and ah's died

123

down across the dining room. Then all went quiet. Horribly quiet. The silence grew thick with tension, only to break up when the poor man announced, "Oh dear! I can't remember who she was."

Do Not Be Afraid

"But the angel said to him, 'Do not be afraid, Zechariah. ... Your wife Elizabeth will bear you a son ...'" (Luke 1:13, NRSV).

"The angel said to her, 'Do not be afraid, Mary ... you will ... bear a son ...'" (Luke 1:30-31, NRSV).

"But the angel said to them [the shepherds], 'Do not be afraid; for see — I am bringing you good news of great joy for all the people: to you is born ... a Savior, who is the Messiah, the Lord'" (Luke 2:10-11, NRSV).

Fear robs us of mirth and joy; the Savior robs us of fear. He does this through His presence. And He comes in a thousand ways — for example, in little children.

Children, nonthreatening in manner, possess sheer magic for putting us at ease. Their carefree spirit of innocence has nothing of adult calculation about it. Adult cleverness and design make us uneasy. The unalloyed motivations of little children sometimes carry right over into adulthood, and when we meet such a person we often stand amazed, feeling tranquil and comfortable.

This is rare; we live in a world of adult manipulation, a money-oriented world.

A university professor sought to itemize reasons why people buy:

(1) Some make purchases on a *rational* basis, saying, "I need this because. ..."

(2) Others procure merchandise for *emotional* reasons.

(3) Still others obtain things out of social *pressure*. Preteens and teens especially respond to "what everybody's got."

(4) Some shop out of *curiosity*. A new item may bring a certain amount of personal satisfaction.

(5) Many procure commodities because of the *situation* — Christmas, a birthday, Mother's Day.

We can never prepare fully for the subtleties invading our lives. Aside from people who try to outwit us, we also fear that the forces of nature or gravity, in storm or accident, will rob us of quality of life, or indeed of life itself.

The Christchild came to put those fears to rest. He is the Savior, Immanuel ("God with us"). And when we associate with little children anywhere, we experience the non-menacing and affirming presence God created us to enjoy.

Children, like Christ, bring not fear but joy unbounded.

Children Make Us Laugh

Jesus loved little children, in part because of their natural ability to bring pleasantry into the flow of life. One suspects Jesus had ability to remove restraints from children so they could be themselves. Fortunately we live in an age unlike earlier eras that announced, "Children are to be seen and not heard."

Don Edwards, a newspaper columnist, writes of the little fellow standing at the bottom of a department store escalator. Intently looking at the handrail, the small boy would not take his eyes away. A salesperson asked, "Are you lost?"

"Nope," came the reply, "I'm waiting for my chewing gum to come back."

The creativity reflected in that little guy, psychologists and researchers now believe, figures more significantly than raw I.Q. as a measure of intelligence. Getzels and Jackson, University of Chicago psychology professors, did research that brought them to this conclusion: giftedness is not really "intelligence," but creativity.

They also concluded, "The outstanding characteristic of the creative child is a sense of humor." Wit and creativity are bedfellows.

Studies involving children and laughter reveal some interesting facts. Babies often laugh first around the 10th week, sometimes earlier. At that age laughter is pretty much reflexive, so their mirthful responses come with surprises and relief.

By the 16th week, they laugh out loud on an hourly basis. One of the most interesting findings is that children learn to translate discomfort, stress and awkward situations into laughter — especially if their parents see the funny side of difficulty. That explains in part why young children refresh us so. They model laughter as tension-release, the very thing we ought to do but frequently avoid! By age four, little ones laugh about every four minutes, usually in the context of their own games, dances and songs.

A British psychologist, David Cohen, discovered that some sounds and touches can trigger laughter between four and six months. He found that by the 10th month, visual and social stimuli can set them laughing — for example, when mother crawls on the floor!

The end of the first year sees children making some of their own fun, inventing their own fantasies. Peek-a-boo, modeled by parents, now takes hold of the child's imagination; he or she may peer around the sofa. At about one year, the child can burlesque, slapping himself on the thigh and pretending, for example, that he is a TV cartoon figure.

Even preschoolers have used humor as a self-critical device. Evidently it also doesn't take long for children to learn to play "sneak" with humor. Some psychologists believe jokes can be subtle aggression against authority figures.

Laughter as an Instrument of Maturation

3

Evidently Jesus' lest-ye-become-as-a-little-child principle reflects more than a humble and open spirit. In fact, the spin-offs are too great to count. But recent research seems to indicate that maturation is one of those by-products, and humor aids the process.

Someone has called catecholamines "alertness hormones." We have already seen that catecholamines, by triggering endorphins (the body's natural painkillers), can reduce aches, discomfort, inflammation, etc. We also know that the brain's receptors open us up to enhanced learning. Relaxation sets in, and that too frees the mind for instruction. Laughter is a practical instrument for education and important to the maturation process.

This relaxation response in laughter has undergone considerable research. One finding concludes that the greater and longer the laugh, the more uptightness diminishes. Tension reduction is a major challenge in the learning/maturation enterprise.

Young children like riddles; older children prefer jokes. Both age groups try their growing vocabulary of words and ideas on older people to get feedback, which can nurture emotional and cognitive growth. Adults tell stories with puns and subtle punch lines, a much more sophisticated genre of humor. So humor sharing becomes a method of learning in the younger, and in adults evidence that mastery has arrived.

Sobriety seems to set in at about middle age, unless individuals program themselves otherwise. Evidently the increased burdens of life tend to diminish the comic elements in our personalities. After retirement the laughter comes back a little, especially in our 70s and 80s. This probably relates to newfound relief from the daily round of responsibilities, coupled with the leisure to see the funny things people do.

But, at any age, one function of laughter seems to be the signaling of wholesome self-regard. And a strong self-image relates closely to what we know as human maturity.

Some research seems to indicate that positive and affirmative facts and experiences return to memory much better if one smiles or laughs. Contrariwise, smiling does not seem to bring back negative details.

4 Communicating Faith in Our Families

That delightful lady, Phyllis McGinley, writes somewhere that in the canonization process, the Catholic church requires proof of joy in the candidate. She admits she cannot cite chapter and verse, but I like the suggestion that sourness is not a sacred attribute.

That mighty spirit, "Praying" Hyde of India, won a reputation for two characteristics: the effectiveness of his intercessions and the hilarity of his laugh. Could the two be related?

Faith makes one contagious. I believe we accept the gift of faith more readily and eagerly when evidenced in those around us. I also believe that children, by nature, avoid someone whose Spartan rigor does not find balance in laughter and the lighter side of life.

Psalms 126:2 (NRSV) has the mark of authenticity about it: "Then our mouth was filled with laughter, and our tongue with shouts of joy; then it was said among the nations, 'The Lord has done great things for them.'"

G.K. Chesterton announced profound truth when he exclaimed, "Joy, which was the small publicity of the pagan, is the gigantic secret of the Christian." Our families look for this gigantic secret. Indeed, everyone searches for it. For it is the secret of Life abundant, what everybody wants.

Families know by our demeanor that the real values in life are not houses, lands and things — these are only instruments. But for contact with reality, they must "see" in the biblical sense. Laughter is one of God's ways of uncovering reality.

Four leading causes of death in our culture are high blood pressure, heart disease, stroke and cancer. Researchers implicate stress in each. We know, for example, that stress worsens these diseases. If laughter, pleasantry and affirming thoughts contribute to alleviation of illness, we have a degree of therapy at our fingertips. And when we take advantage of this healing power, we project the life of faith to our households.

Whenever faith finds creative and positive expression, know this: its nature is contagion. Holy contagion.

Dropping Cares

Psalms 94:19 reads, "When the cares of my heart are many, your consolations cheer my soul" (NRSV). And 1 Peter 5:7 tells us to cast our anxieties on God because he cares for us.

Have you heard the story of the two Japanese monks? Traveling a muddy road, a downpour only added to the difficulty of walking. Around a bend in the road, they met a lovely girl in flowing silk kimono, unable to cross the intersection. Immediately the monk, Tanzan, took the girl in his arms and carried her through the mud and onto more secure ground.

The monks continued their hike, but the other monk, Ekido, spoke not a word until they reached their temple lodgings at night. Now he restrained himself no longer: "We monks never go near females," he remonstrated with Tanzan; "most particularly not young and pretty ones." Ekido had to say more: "It is dangerous, so why did you do it?"

"I left the girl there," replied Tanzan in a quiet spirit. "Are *you* still carrying her?"

The touch of humor in that little story rings with wisdom. Unloading cares and temptations, decisions past and future, come a lot easier with a bit of glee.

Simon Tugwell, who tells the story of the two monks, indicates that "we must learn to pass through situations like a fish, rather than carrying them all with us like a snail." A too-intense attention to life's experiences can drain spirit and emotions. To nurture the art of unloading, without shirking responsibility, is a significant secret of happy living.

Why carry more with us than we need to? Each life event carries quite enough challenge by itself! This is especially relevant to our family life, for there we have our chief investment and intensity mounts quickly.

Good news: God will help us cast cares on Him because He cares for us.

6 Antidote to Cynicism

"When he entered the house," according to Matthew 9:28 (NRSV), "the blind men came to him; and Jesus said to them, 'Do you believe that I am able to do this?' They said to him, 'Yes, Lord.'" Belief is the vehicle for healing, cynicism is its enemy.

Some laughter fosters distrust. Tragically, it is the very laughter that ultimately destroys laughter itself. But that need not be the case. Attitude is a choice.

Marian Diamond, University of California, discovered that we human beings never outgrow our childhood. Children believe naturally; whereas, cynicism is an adult accretion. So we have nature on our side to help us decide for belief.

Diamond discovered from her research that we need never stop learning. We can always submit to needed and progressive change if we will. Perhaps best of all, we can decide to keep laughing.

One of the key factors nudging us to decide for childlike belief is what we see in the modeled home. As kids grow to adulthood and have to wrestle with the hassles of life, cynicism has an insidious way of taking hold. Disappointments, reverses and difficulties can produce a defeatist mind-set, especially if negativism has characterized one's homelife in the early years. That, in turn, often eventually yields the stinking flower called burnout.

But Frudenberger and North, in their book on *Women's Burnout*, make this interesting observation: "Very few people suffer burnout when they're having fun." The two researchers summarize 12 ways to avoid burnout, and the 12th is to nurture and maintain your sense of humor.

If cynicism easily becomes habitual, so does wholesome laughter. And the latter is more contagious than the former! More, a spirit of fun possesses the capacity to halt cynicism in its earliest stages.

Best Friends

"A good wife who can find?" asks the writer of Proverbs 31. "She is far more precious than jewels" (v. 10, RSV). Verse 11 gives a reason: "The heart of her husband trusts in her. ..." And there lies the basis of the most intimate friendship, the friendship we call marriage.

Later in that remarkable chapter of Proverbs, which hails the hallmarks of the good wife, the writer says "she laughs at the time to come" (v. 25). She does not worry about tomorrow; she can laugh because strength and dignity clothe her, because she tackles the duties of life with courage and forthrightness. Whatever happens, this woman faces life prepared.

Francis Bacon observed that, "There is no man that imparteth his joys to his friends, but he joyeth the more; and no man that imparteth his griefs to his friend, but he grieveth the less." The same holds true with husband and wife, with children and parents. Confrontation with life in the family unit requires genuine love, and joy is the child of love.

When this kind of honest-to-goodness friendship exists in the family, what others do has a way of carrying interest and excitement. Crafts and projects, money tallying and usage, yard care and house maintenance, meal preparation and cleaning up after eating — all have about them the earmark of mutual effort and the sense of joyous reward.

The family's eating experiences can be enriched by the joy of storytelling, sharing the day's events, wholesome give-and-take in the grand enterprise of learning, joking and ribbing of one another. All these little love signs spell warmth and deep joy, and bring peace and well-being.

William Hazlitt rightly said we cannot force friendship any more than we can force love. But we do know some things that will foster friendship and love in the family. We can focus on Christ, the source of joy; we can concentrate on positive experiences. Even when we must empty our souls of negatives, the family can listen with support. And affirmation blossoms into joy.

Families that cultivate one another as best friends also reflect God's available grace for creating peace and joy.

XIII

Sources for the Renewal of Joy

"For, lo, the winter is past,
the rain is over and gone;
the flowers appear on the earth;
the time of the singing
of birds is come,
and the voice of the turtle
is heard in our land."
—Song of Solomon 2:11-12, KJV

Have a Good Laugh

The third grade teacher asked her students to write about their summer vacations. One little girl said she and her family had gone to Hawaii. The blue sky, the water falls, the dancers and the cookouts — all pleased her a great deal.

A little boy recorded that he and his family went to Washington, D.C. They saw the Washington Monument, both houses of Congress, and had a tour of the White House.

A third said he did not go very far or have many unusual experiences, but he did visit his grandfather's farm. He liked milking and harvesting and farm meals. But one funny sight puzzled him: All those little pigs trying to blow up that big pig.

1 The Primary Source

In Psalm 100, replete with joy, we read:

Shout for joy to the Lord, all the earth.
Serve the Lord with gladness;
*   come before Him with joyful songs.*
Know that the Lord is God.
It is He who made us, and we are his;
*   we are his people, the sheep of his*
*   pasture.*
Enter his gates with thanksgiving
*   and his courts with praise;*
*   give thanks to him and praise his name.*
For the Lord is good and his love endures forever;
*   his faithfulness continues through*
*   all generations.* (NIV)

In that exuberant piece of poetry we see the secrets of renewed joy. (1) Knowledge that the Lord is God. The ancient writer Marcianus Aristides observed that, "God is not in need of anything, but all things are in need of Him." God stands supreme, in charge of everything; God is Creator. The sure knowledge that God *is* God is the primary source of security and, therefore, renewed joy.

(2) The second secret comes on the heels of the first: God is good. Lady Julian of Norwich saw the relation of the two secrets: "Some of us believe that God is Almighty and may do all, and that he is All-wisdom and can do all; but that he is All-love and will do all — there we stop short."

God is indeed good. Good, mind you, not merely in

theory, but in terms of His involvement in the world, in you and me, and in all His children. That good, says our Psalm, endures forever. Put in practical language, His faithfulness goes on from generation to generation, to my children and grandchildren.

One further truth about this Psalm: it's couched in a spirit of unadulterated thankfulness. Said Izaak Walton, "God has two dwellings — one in heaven and the other in a thankful heart." Well now, since God cannot possibly divorce Himself from joy, the heart captured by Him owns gladness.

How to renew yourself in joy? Seek God and find Him.

Suffering and Joy

2

St. Paul, in one of his soaring moments, declared, "No, in all these things we are more than conquerors through him who loved us. For I am convinced that neither death, nor life, nor angels, nor rulers, nor things present, nor things to come, nor powers, nor height, nor depth, nor anything else in all creation, will be able to separate us from the love of God in Christ Jesus our Lord" (Romans 8:37-39, NRSV).

Here Paul triumphs over tragedy. He never once tries to avoid the hard fact of suffering; indeed, he seems to see it as opportunity to overcome with zest. Humor and joy often come out of raw suffering. Sincere laughter and authentic joy relate to all of life, including hardship.

You will notice at once that St. Paul does not entertain fears of suffering. Said a wise man, "What is unbearable is not to suffer but to be afraid of suffering." Fearful persons, as in athletic experiences, miss half the game and thereby rob themselves of fulfillment and joy.

To accept suffering as part of life is a great freedom. That leads us to another liberating truth, a truth couched by Simone Weil, the French mystic: "It is in affliction itself that the splendor of God's mercy shines. ..."

Mother Teresa knows this truth, for she says that

135

God is closest to the poorest of the poor. Jesus talked about the blessedness, the happiness, of the poor in spirit.

Baron von Hugel saw this clearly when he observed, "Suffering is the great teacher." He even says we have our value system all wrong, that "suffering is the crown of life." He explains by this exclamation: "Suffering and expansion [another term for education], what a rich combination!" Von Hugel goes on: "All deepened life is deepened suffering, deepened dreariness, deepened joy. Suffering and joy. The final note of religion is joy."

Suffering refines us, peals off the layers of selfishness, shoves us into a hurting world to mend its wounds, and above all teaches us something of the meaning of the cross of Christ. When all that begins to take shape in our thinking, we find ourselves.

Alexander Solzhenitsyn said of his experience in the Russian prison camp, that there he discovered his soul. He, like Paul, can thank God for suffering. This accounts for the joy in both men.

3 Growing Faith

St. Paul's personal joy overflows as he addresses the Christians at Thessalonica: "We must always give thanks to God for you, brothers and sisters as is right, because your faith is growing abundantly, and the love of everyone of you for one another is increasing." He goes on to talk about "faith during all your persecutions and in the afflictions which you are enduring" (2 Thessalonians 1:3-4, NRSV). Clearly these early Christians grew in that all-important life component, faith.

This is a tricky business, for the world conditions us to believe that happiness lies in mere pleasure, the transitory, the sensual. Although things possess potential for good, raw worldly gratification is a dead-end street. This explains William Wordsworth's cogent words in *The Prelude*:

> Not in Utopia, — subterranean fields, —

> *Or some secreted island, Heaven knows where!*
> *But in the very world, which is the world*
> *Of all of us, — the place where, in the end,*
> *We find our happiness, or not at all!*

In other words, authentic gladness comes from within yourself. Put more fully, it stems from sturdy developing faith.

Mary Asquith helps us think clearly about faith: "There is a difference between a good, sound reason for our faith, and a reason that sounds good." Shallow faith, like a tree rotted inside, blows over in the storms of persecution and affliction.

Even the classic writers on Utopia seemed to have understood this. The very word *Utopia* means "No place." William Norris did a book called *News From Nowhere*, but Samuel Butler did one called *Erehwon*, NOWHERE spelled backwards.

Jesus said the kingdom of God (faith) lives in us (Luke 17:21) and that it had come with Him. The source of true happiness is His kingdom. When that kingdom lives in us by Christ's Spirit, faith reigns.

Now that faith, that kingdom of joy, needs periodic refurbishing. How do we do that? "We are not called upon to renew our minds in order that we may be transfigured," said William L. Pettingill; "we are only to yield ourselves unto God, and he does all the rest."

And what is this "all the rest?" Ah! Christopher Morley had it right: "April prepares her green traffic light and the world thinks go."

Temple Gairdner talked well of renewal's reality: "That sense of newness is simply delicious. It makes new the Bible and friends, and all mankind and love and spiritual things and Sunday and church and God Himself." Now that's real joy!

Fulfilling Work

The book of Proverbs tells us that we should "commit" our work "to the Lord;" then our "plans will be established" (16:3, NRSV). Applied, that proverb means that when we labor with noble purpose and achieve something worthwhile, we experience deep satisfaction, real joy.

My friend, Dr. Kenneth Kinghorn, feels this way after completing a writing project, even one unit of a project. If, he says, he can end a workday knowing he has been productive, that's about as good a feeling as he ever comes by. And the completion of a whole book brings decided gratification.

The clue to that sense of well-being comes from committing your work "to the Lord." So Martin Luther observed that, "A dairymaid can milk cows to the glory of God." Once one believes his or her efforts center in honoring God, pride in quality productivity enters the soul.

George MacDonald, that unusual Scottish storyteller who influenced C.S. Lewis, remarked that, "It is our best work that He [God] wants, not the dregs of our exhaustion. I think He must prefer quality to quantity." There you have one of the big secrets of fulfillment, for we intuitively know that excellence supersedes mere quantity. We know that well, despite our emphasis on mass production programs and the planned obsolescence that goes with a high-tech economy.

Quality demands hard work. Not joyless labor, but diligence. One writer revises a dozen times; the rule of thumb in journalistic circles is five, but he will not find satisfaction with ordinary editing.

Michelangelo called details "trifles," and then observed that "perfection is no trifle."

"If people knew how hard I work to get my mastery," he once said, "it wouldn't seem so wonderful after all." But, oh! How wonderful to aim for quality! And how extraordinary any person's creativity is in God's sight when done with care.

Somehow the knowledge of God's approval gives us that special kick we get out of exertion. William Lyon Phelps, Yale professor of English, used to say he wished he could pay for the privilege of teaching. Walter Muelder, longtime dean of Boston University Divinity School, said his work was just plain fun. When work is fun it rejuvenates, contributes to wholeness, and points to God.

The bottom line: work itself can renew joy in the human spirit.

Leisure and Creative Experience

Jesus announced truth with unsurpassed beauty and meaning. On one occasion He gave this counsel: "Come to me, all you that are weary and are carrying heavy burdens, and I will give you rest. Take my yoke upon you, and learn from me; for I am gentle and humble in heart, and you will find rest for your souls. For my yoke is easy, and my burden is light" (Matthew 11:28-30, NRSV).

Edgar W. Howe, putting his finger on one of the ways we rob ourselves of joy, said, "It's no credit to anyone to work too hard." Any attempt to project feelings of the "heavy laden" syndrome falls short of God's will.

An important source of joy is taking time off so we can return to work with zest, enthusiasm and purpose. The trick lies in putting experiences of creative substance in those times off.

Some will go to a bookstore. Not a bad idea, for in a really good one the browser surveys an art gallery in miniature. Even modern book jackets reflect a whole genre of artistic expression.

Children's books take us into an art world of their own, a world that says we live in a renaissance of children's literature and drawing. The classics section of the store reminds us of hope and idealism and thus restores our faith in God, others and life. The very arrangement of the books by sections, the overall visual impact, has in itself a renewing effect. Books are friends that invigorate us.

Some will migrate not to a bookstore but to a concert and get their fill of great music, silver-toned sounds with power to restore the soul. Others will go out into nature — to a park for a picnic, to a lake to fish, to the mountains to watch God paint His sunsets. Still others will join friends with mutual interests at a dinner party, where the talk and good food play their revitalizing roles.

Workaholism is a thief, a deceiver who only wears the mask of joy. Periodic leisure, filled with rewarding stimulation, restores the imaginative powers, making the daily round not just bearable but exalted with true dignity and joyous reality.

Friends

The book of Proverbs has a way of couching truth in few words. For example, "A friend loves at all times, and kinsfolk are born to share adversity" (17:17, NRSV).

Samuel Johnson, in his inimitable way, declared that, "If a man does not make new acquaintances as he advances through life, he will soon find himself left alone. A man, sir, should keep his friendship in constant repair."

The necessity for friends finds documentation in the very flow of life. Few joys surpass friendship. Essays, indeed whole books on the subject, have come to publication.

No recent research stands out more eloquently than the study of over 7,000 who suffered such cataclysmic diseases as cancer and vascular problems. Recorded in the *American Journal of Epidemiology*, the essential finding is this: those who enjoyed a strong support system of friends and family survived at a much higher rate than those without such a system.

We know some of the reasons for that: friends bring joy and enthusiasm, a certain verve and pizzazz characterized by stories, laughter and general well-being. All that, we also know, kicks antibodies into action, enhancing the endocrine and hormonal systems to stave off or reverse disease. In other words, the support system created by friends and family activates the body's own therapy and support systems.

The source of friendship is God. An amazing passage in Exodus reads: "Thus the Lord used to speak to Moses face to face, as a man speaks to a friend" (33:11, NRSV). That kind of relationship with God fosters therapy and guidance. And once we establish that fundamental relationship, human friends come naturally, for people migrate toward the wholesomeness God engenders.

Charles F. Andrews bears testimony to the power of friendship with God: "The older I grow in years, the more the wonder and the joy increase when I see the power of these words of Jesus — 'I have called you friends' — to move the human heart. That one word 'friend' breaks down each barrier of reserve, and we have boldness in his presence." He concludes: "Our hearts go out in love to meet his love." That love defines the wholesomeness which brings friends.

Now, then, who can possibly know the love of God and human friends and remain destitute of joy?

The Retreat Experience

Psalms 116:7 reads, "Return, O my soul, to your rest, for the Lord has dealt bountifully with you" (NRSV). The word *rest* occurs frequently in Scripture. God rested on the seventh day; Jesus invited His friends to come away to rest; the book of Hebrews refers to it repeatedly; we find it in Genesis, Exodus and other places.

The function of a retreat is rest, the restoration of mind and body along with the spiritual and emotional refurbishing that comes in a well-thought-out-program. Fortunately we live in an age of opportunities for spiri-

tual renewal. Leaving telephone, mailbox, fax, computer
and routine paves the way for opening the soul to fresh
messages from God, self and others. These dispatches
flow with astonishing frequency once we quiet ourselves
to listen.

Henry Vaughan, 17th-century writer, captures the
therapy of retreat under the figure of night:

> *Dear Night: this world's defeat;*
> *The stop to busy fools; care's check and curb;*
> *The day of spirits; my soul's calm retreat*
> *Which none can disturb!*

The absence of that undisturbed calm issues inevitably in the draining off of joy. And the reverse holds true:
The inspiration of silence restores the glad heart.

But we must know how to use silence. Thus the
necessity of the well-structured retreat. We must have
leaders who stimulate our minds with probing questions
and comforting, strengthening commentary on life. We
must have group sharing that invites the Spirit of God to
wash over our souls like green fields and still waters. And
the pace and periods between talk must come often to
permit that refreshing wash.

Retreats do not cost that much, but the interest on
the investment is a hundredfold. Encourage yourself to
attend the next available retreat. Work toward such a
program in your church and community. Stir enthusiasm
after a spiritual getaway by offering public witness to its
benefits. With retreat centers covering the nation, leaders
in abundance, experts on camping, the specialist knowledge we now possess about small-group dynamics, and
the wide range of themes for spiritual encounter — well,
the sky's the limit! And unbounded too, the renewed joy
retreats bring.

Bibliography

Allen, Steve. *How to Make A Speech*. New York: McGraw-Hill, 1986.

_____. *Funny People*. New York: Stein and Day, 1981.

Armour, Richard. *It All Started with Freshmen English*. New York: McGraw-Hill, 1973.

Barclay, William. *Daily Celebration*, Vol. 2. Edited by Denis Duncan. Waco: Word Books, 1974.

Basset, Elizabeth. editor, with Foreword by her Majesty Queen Elizabeth the Queen Mother. *Love Is My Meaning: An Anthology of Assurance*. Atlanta: John Knox Press, 1974.

"Becoming Fools for Christ: Clowning as an Aid to Holy Ritual and Service." *Time*, September 1, 1980.

Berger, Peter. *A Rumor of Angels*. Garden City: Doubleday, 1969.

Bishop, George. *The World of Clowns*. Los Angeles: Brooke House, 1976.

Bonner, Philip. "A Legacy of Excellence and Humor." *Sky*, October 1990. N. Miami, FL: Halsey Publishing Co.

Book of Common Prayer. New York: Harper, 1944.

Brengle, Samuel Logan. *Resurrection Life and Power*. Atlanta: The Salvation Army Supplies and Purchasing Dept., 1981 reprint.

_____. *Helps to Holiness*. Atlanta: The Salvation Army Supplies and Purchasing Dept., 1981 reprint.

Brody, Robert. "Anatomy of a Laugh." *American Health*, November/December 1983.

Buechner, Frederick. *Telling the Truth: The Gospel As Tragedy, Comedy, and Fairy Tale*. San Francisco: Harper, 1977.

Buffington, Perry W. "Make 'Em Laugh." *Sky*, April 1984, N. Miami, FL: Halsey Publishing Co.

Bullock, Alan and Oliver Stallybrass, editors. *The Harper Dictionary of Modern Thought*. New York: Harper, 1977.

Burns, George. *How to Live to Be One Hundred — or More*. New York: G.P. Putnam's Sons, 1983.

Buscaglia, Leo. *Loving Each Other: The Challenge of Human Relationships*. New York: Holt, Rinehart and Winston, 1984.

"Clown College." *National Geographic World*, September 1982.

Cousins, Norman. *Anatomy of an Illness as Perceived by the Patient*. New York: W.W. Norton & Co., 1979.

Cosby, Bill. *Fatherhood*. New York: Doubleday, 1986.

Demaray, Donald E. *Watch Out for Burnout*. Grand Rapids: Baker Book House, 1983.

Dieter, Melvin E. *The Christian's Secret of a Holy Life: The Unpublished Personal Writings of Hannah Whitall Smith*. Grand Rapids: Zondervan, 1994.

Donahue, Phil. *The Human Animal*. New York: Simon and Schuster, 1985.

Edwards, Don. "Bright Christmas." *Lexington (Kentucky) Herald-Leader*, December 19, 1985, B 1.

Elias, Marilyn. "Be Upbeat and Beat Illness, Stress." *USA Today*, August 26, 1985, Section D, p.1.

Esar, Evan. *Esar's Comic Dictionary*. Garden City: Doubleday, 1983.

Farris, John T. *The Book of Joy*. London: Hodder and Stoughton, 1917.

Foster, Richard J. and James Bryan Smith, editors. *Devotional Classics*. San Francisco: Harper, 1993.

Freudenberger, Herbert J. and Gail North. *Women's Burnout*. Garden City: Doubleday, 1985.

Fry, William F., Jr. *Sweet Madness: A Study of Humor*. Palo Alto, California: Pacific Books, 1963.

Gaebelein, Frank E. *The Christian, The Arts, and Truth*. Portland, Oregon: Multnomah Press, 1985.

Gossip, Arthur John. *In the Secret Place of the Most High Being Some Studies in Prayer*. London: Independent Press, 1946.

Green, Roger Lancelyn and Walter Hooper. *C.S. Lewis: A Biography*. New York: Harcourt Brace Jovanovich, 1974.

Hall, Clarence W. *Samuel Logan Brengle: Portrait of a Prophet*. Atlanta: The Salvation Army Supplies and Purchasing Dept., 1979 reprint.

Herbert, Sir Alan. "The English Laugh." (The English Association Presidential Address) Oxford: University Press, 1950.

"Hilarity." *Weavings: A Journal of the Christian Spiritual Life*. Nashville: Upper Room, Fall 1994.

Jennison, Keith W. *The Humorous Mr. Lincoln*. New York: Bonanza Books, 1965.

Job, Rueben P. and Norman Shawchuck, editors. *A Guide to Prayer for Ministers and Other Servants*. Nashville: The Upper Room, 1983.

John Paul II, Pope. *Crossing the Threshold of Hope*. New York: Alfred A. Knopf, 1994.

Johnson, Janice. "Laughs Every Day Could Keep the Doctor Away." *USA Weekend*, Nov. 22-24, 1985.

"Joyful Noises." *Christianity Today*. November 14, 1994, p. 46.

Kavanaugh, Patrick. *The Spiritual Lives of Great Composers*. Nashville: Sparrow Press, 1992.

Kidder, Rushworth M. "TV Has Turned Public Discussion into 'Sea of Amusements.'" *Lexington (Kentucky) Herald-Leader*, November 26, 1985 (editorial page).

King, Duncan and Angela Akers. *Amusing Grace: Humor to Heal Mind, Soul and Body*. Sevenworlds Corp.: Knoxville, 1993.

Knille, Robert, editor. *As I was Saying ... A Chesterton Reader*. Grand Rapids: Eerdmans, 1985.

"Laugh Yourself to Health." *The Indianapolis Star*, October 30, 1977, section 3.
"Laughing Away Dental Fears." *Prevention*, December 1984, p. 9.
"Laughing Toward Longevity." *Wellness Letter*, June 1985. Berkeley: University of California School of Public Health.
"Laughs Every Day Could Keep the Doctor Away." *USA Weekend*, November 22-24, 1985.
"Laughter Heals: Positive Thoughts Are a Potent Cure." *The Seattle Times*, May 21, 1983.
"Laughter *IS* the Best Medicine." *Reader's Digest*, April 1985, p. 47.
Laymen, Fred D. "Theology and Humor." *The Asbury Seminarian*, Winter, 1982-83. Wilmore, Kentucky: Asbury Theological Seminary.
Lewis, C.S. *Surprised by Joy: The Shape of My Early Life*. New York: Harcourt Brace and Company, 1955.
Lloyd-Jones, Martyn. *Joy Unspeakable: Power and Renewal in the Holy Spirit*. Edited by Christopher Catherwood. Wheaton: Harold Shaw, 1984.
McGhee, Paul E. and Jeffrey Goldstein. *Handbook of Humor Research*. Vol. 2, *Applied Studies*. New York: Springer-Verlag, 1983.
Meisel, Martin. "Oscar Wilde," *World Book*, Vol. 21. (Chicago: Field Enterprises Educational Corporation, 1975), p. 254.
"Members Request for Humor Brought Avalanche of Ideas." *AARP News Bulletin*, April 1985.
Merton, Thomas. *No Man Is an Island*. New York: Harcourt Brace Jovanovich Publishers, 1983 (renewed copyright).
Minirth, Frank B., M.D. and Paul D. Meier, M.D. with Foreword by Paul Tournier. *Happiness Is a Choice: A Manual on the Symptoms, Causes, and Cures of Depression*. Grand Rapids: Baker Book House, 1978.
Moody, Raymond A., M.D. *Laugh After Laugh: The Healing Power of Humor*. Jackson, Florida: Headwaters Press, 1978.
Morrice, William, with Foreword by A.M. Hunter. *Joy in the New Testament*. Grand Rapids: Eerdmans, 1984.
Mullen, Tom. *Laughing Out Loud and Other Religious Experiences*. Waco: Word Books, 1983.
Mullen, Wilbur. "Toward A Theology of Humor." *Christian Scholar's Review*, March, 1973.
Myra, Harold L. "A Message from the Publisher." *Christianity Today*, December 13, 1985, p. 17.
Oliver, Robert T. *The Psychology of Persuasive Speech*. New York: David McKay, 1957 (second edition).
Parrott, Bob W. *God's Sense of Humor —Where? When? How?* New York: Philosophical Library, 1984.
Peale, Norman Vincent. *How to Make Jesus Your Best Friend*. Pawling, New York: Peale Center for Christian Living, 1991.
_____. *The True Joy of Positive Living: An*

Autobiograpy. Carmel New York: Guideposts, 1984.

_____. *This Incredible Century.* Pawling, New York: Peale Center for Christian Living, 1991.

_____. *Treasure of Joy and Enthusiasm.* Pawling, New York: Foundation for Christian Living, 1981.

_____. "When Loved Ones Leave Us." *Plus,* March 1985, Pawling, New York: Foundation for Christian Living.

Peter, Laurence J. *The Laughter Prescription: How to Achieve Health, Happiness, and Peace of Mind Through Humor.* New York: Ballantine, 1982.

Peters, Thomas J. and Robert H. Waterman, Jr. *In Search of Excellence.* New York: Harper, 1982.

Peterson, Eugene H. *A Long Obedience in the Same Direction.* Downers Grove: Inter-Varsity, 1980.

Postman, Neil. *Amusing Ourselves to Death: Public Disclosure in the Age of Showbusiness.* New York: Viking Press, 1985.

Raskin, Victor. "Jokes: A Linguist Explains His New Semantic Theory of Humor." *Psychology Today,* October 1985.

Richie, Charles. "Humor ... in Christian Living." *Evangelical Beacon,* November 25, 1985.

Rohrer, Norman B. *Leighton Ford: A Life Surprised.* Wheaton: Tyndale House, 1981.

Schlink, Mother Basilea. *Repentance —the Joy-Filled Life.* Minneapolis: Bethany House Publishers, 1984.

Smith, Jane Stuart and Betty Carlson. *A Gift of Music: Great Composers and Their Influence.* Westchester, Illinois: Cornerstone Books, 1979.

Spangler, Ann, editor. *Bright Legacy: Portraits of Ten Outstanding Christian Women.* Ann Arbor: Servant Books, 1983.

Teichman, Howard. "The Brave Journey of Helen Hayes." *Parade,* November 24, 1985.

The Joyful Noiseletter: Epistle of the Fellowship of Merry Christians. A Periodical published at Portage, Michigan: P.O. Box 895, 49081-0895.

Tournier, Paul. "The Blessings of a Deep Loss." *Christianity Today,* November 23, 1984, pp. 28-9.

Trueblood, Elton. *The Humor of Christ.* New York: Harper, 1975, Jubilee reprint.

Turner, Dale E. *Words of Wisdom and Other Columns.* Seattle: The Seattle Times, n.d.

Tuttle, Lee F. *Profiles of 20th Century Pulpit Giants: From Personal Acquaintance.* Published in 1984 by the author in Lake Junaluska, N.C.

Wallis, Charles L., editor. *The Treasure Chest.* New York: Harper, 1965.

Wilde, Oscar. *The Importance of Being Earnest.* Edited by Vincent F. Hopper and Gerald B. Lahey with note of the staging by George L. Hershey and illustrations by Fritz Kredel. Woodbury,

New York: Barron's Educational Series, n.d.

Will, George F. "Dickens' Emphasis Was on Individual." *Lexington (Kentucky) Herald-Leader*, November 29, 1985.

Willimon, William H. *And the Laugh Shall Be First: A Treasure of Religious Humor.* Nashville: Abingdon, 1980.

Woods, Ralph L., compiler. *Friendship.* Norwalk, Connecticut: C.R. Gibson Co., 1969.

Yancey, Philip. "From Carnival to Mardi Gras." *Christianity Today*, April 26, 1993, p. 64.